■ ■ ■

George Barna has done it again. He is touching at the heart of the evangelical mission and does so with insight and skill. I've never been disappointed by one of Barna's books, and this book proves to be another winner.

JOE C. ALDRICH
*President, Multnomah Bible College and Biblical Seminary*
*Portland, Oregon*

■ ■ ■

Offering more than an analysis of the problem, Barna points the way to church renewal and effective outreach to the lost. Here is power-packed research that evangelizers dare not ignore.

ROBERT E. COLEMAN
*Director, School of World Mission and Evangelism,*
*Trinity Evangelical Divinity School*
*Deerfield, Illinois*

■ ■ ■

George Barna is absolutely right that our postmodern American culture is increasingly resistant to traditional programs of evangelistic outreach. His greatest concern is for the lack of spiritual passion and compassion among Christians for those who don't belong to Christ. In this book, Barna shares both his research and his heart. It is important to hear both.

ROBERT A. FRYLING
*Vice President and Director of Campus Ministries,*
*InterVarsity Christian Fellowship*
*Madison, Wisconsin*

■ ■ ■

This book is a must for those who want to turn talk into action.

THE REV. EDDIE GIBBS
*Associate Rector for Discipleship, All Saints' Parish,*
*The Episcopal Church in Beverly Hills*
*Beverly Hills, California*

■ ■ ■

Here is the overflow of a Christian leader's impassioned heart—pointing with humbled concern to the fact that a blinded and bound society is damned and helpless. Here's help for seeing and thinking clearly—so you and I can reach them, one by one, with discerning and loving effectiveness.

**JACK W. HAYFORD**
*Senior Pastor, The Church On The Way*
*Van Nuys, California*

■  ■  ■

George Barna has combined powerful research and deep passion to send every believer, every church a wake-up call from God. If we hear his message, it will change our lives and our neighbors' eternity.

**RON HUTCHCRAFT**
*Author, Speaker and Radio Host*
*Wayne, New Jersey*

■  ■  ■

Those who are committed to evangelism must read this book. Read it! Think on it! It's a great addition to the cause of evangelism today.

**DOUG MURREN**
*Pastor, Eastside Foursquare Church*
*Kirkland, Washington*

■  ■  ■

George Barna has hit another home run. No pastor who is serious about reaching unsaved people can ignore this book or turn a deaf ear to its conclusions.

**ELMER L. TOWNS**
*Dean, School of Religion, Liberty University*
*Lynchburg, Virginia*

■  ■

# GEORGE BARNA

# EVANGELISM THAT WORKS

# GEORGE BARNA

AUTHOR OF *USER FRIENDLY CHURCHES* AND *THE FROG IN THE KETTLE*

# EVANGELISM
# THAT WORKS

HOW TO REACH CHANGING
GENERATIONS WITH THE
UNCHANGING GOSPEL

**Regal Books**
A Division of Gospel Light
Ventura, California, U.S.A.

Regal Books
A Division of Gospel Light
Ventura, California, U.S.A.
Printed in U.S.A.

Regal Books is a ministry of Gospel Light, an evangelical Christian publisher dedicated to serving the local church. We believe God's vision for Gospel Light is to provide church leaders with
biblical, user-friendly materials that will help them evangelize, disciple and minister to children,
youth and families.

It is our prayer that this Regal Book will help you discover biblical truth for your own life and
help you meet the needs of others. May God richly bless you.

For a free catalog of resources from Regal Books/Gospel Light please contact your Christian supplier or
call 1-800-4-GOSPEL.

**Library of Congress Cataloging-in-Publication Data**
Barna, George.
    Evangelism that works / George Barna.
        p. cm.
    Includes bibliographical references (p. ).
    ISBN 0-8307-1739-0 (hardcover)
    1. Evangelistic work. I. Title.
BV3790.B328 1995                                                    95-11788
269'2—dc20                                                              CIP

1  2  3  4  5  6  7  8  9  10  11  12  /  02  01  00  99  98  97  96  95

Rights for publishing this book in other languages are contracted by Gospel Literature International
(GLINT). GLINT also provides technical help for the adaptation, translation and publishing of Bible
study resources and books in scores of languages worldwide. For further information, contact GLINT
P.O. Box 4060, Ontario, CA 91761-1003, U.S.A., or the publisher.

# CONTENTS

■ ■ ■ ■ ■ ■ ■ ■ ■ ■ ■ ■ ■ ■ ■

This is *not* a book of theology, doctrine or statistics. It is the story of a universal community of faith known as the Church that is called to evangelize, and it describes the current state of affairs and where we may be heading, spiritually.

Americans who have failed to find happiness in bigger homes, fatter paychecks and more leisure time are searching for spiritual truths that would free them from the shackles of worldliness.

Although the United States has been bombarded with the gospel through radio, television, film, newspapers and evangelists, many people have failed to absorb it, to understand it or to embrace it.

Many nonbelievers who failed to find meaningful answers to concerns about "quality of life" and "real life" issues have abandoned the Church but might be enticed to return.

To effectively market a church, the people in the church must develop caring relationships with the nonchurched, and the Church must sponsor nonreligious events that appeal to outsiders.

Although the typical church is only moderately involved in reaching nonbelievers, millions of people each year share their faith through lifestyle evangelism and other forms of evangelism.

■  ■

# ACKNOWLEDGMENTS

I have yet to write a book in which all of the credit should go to me. It must be shared with those to whom it is due. Sometimes people deserve credit because they have shaped my understanding of the subject matter. Sometimes they are noteworthy because they have provided needed encouragement. In other cases, they should share the spotlight because they have sacrificed a part of their lives to see the book to birth. I wish to acknowledge the support of all three types of people.

I have the privilege of working with two of these special entities. The Barna Research Group, Ltd. is a dedicated group of God's servants seeking to assist ministries with current insights into the people those ministries hope to serve. During the days when I squirrelled away to write this book and during the research process itself, my colleagues were of immense help. I particularly wish to thank Nancy Barna, Brian Gammill, Gwen Ingram, George Maupin and Pam Turner for their support, encouragement and prayers.

Similarly, in my work at New Venture Christian Fellowship, a group of gifted and committed ministers and staff members serve a large and growing congregation of God's people. I especially would like to thank Heather Bliss, Andre Brackens, Greg Chastain, Pastor Shawn Mitchell, Gary VanDerford, Tom Woods and the rest of the team for their part in teaching me more about ministry and for their prayers for this work.

As always, my team at Regal Books has been a major source of motivation and enlightenment. Since we began producing ministry resources together several years ago, the relationship has been growing wonderfully. A strong, enjoyable and productive partnership has materialized. Although the cast is large, I am especially grateful to Kyle Duncan, Bill Greig Jr., Bill Greig III, Dennis Somers, Bill Denzel, Barbara LeVan Fisher, Gloria Moss, Virginia Woodard and Gary Greig for their efforts in making this book come alive. Their belief in the work of Barna Research and their personal kindness to me have been a reflection of the Christian ideal.

I am proud to be associated with the tremendous people at Barna Research, New Venture and Gospel Light.

But words do not describe my appreciation and love for the three women who have enabled me most to continue this work, who have been a continual source of energy and support and who have prayed for me daily.

My wife, Nancy, is not a writer, and after watching me stay up through the night on numerous occasions to finish a chapter or to agonize over a concept, she has no interest in becoming one. But she has been my keenest supporter, my most constructive critic and my most understanding sympathizer for nearly two decades. She once again sacrificed much as this book was being created.

My daughter Samantha, although only three years old, also encouraged me in this effort through her concern, her questions, her prayers and her love of life. And during the development of this book, we were blessed with the arrival of our second daughter, Corban. She, too, has played a unique role in my perspective of life, eternity and God's love.

I can imagine nothing more horrifying than to think that any of these special people might spend eternity living apart from God. I thank Him that Nancy is safely nestled in His palm. I pray that as Samantha and Corban become older, they, too, will know the unspeakable peace and honor of knowing Jesus Christ personally. That is what this book is about. I could pray for nothing less than salvation for my daughters. And I pray the same for all people who have yet to realize that Jesus Christ is their one and only hope.

# INTRODUCTION

Though I am free and belong to no man, I make myself a slave to everyone, to win as many as possible. To the Jews I became like a Jew, to win the Jews. To those under the law I became like one under the law (though I myself am not under the law), so as to win those under the law. To those not having the law I became like one not having the law (though I am not free from God's law but am under Christ's law), so as to win those not having the law. To the weak I became weak, to win the weak. I have become all things to all men so that *by all possible means* I might save some. I do all this for the sake of the gospel, that I may share in its blessings (1 Cor. 9:19-23, italics added).

## WHICH TRAGEDY IS THE BIGGEST?

Let's play the child's game, "Big, Bigger, Biggest."

This year, 2.2 million people will die in America.[1] Their passing will lead to months of grieving by tens of thousands of family members and friends. To them, the death of 2.2 million people will be a *big tragedy.*

Only God knows how many of those people who die will wind up in a state of eternal separation from Him, which we commonly refer to as hell. Research suggests, however, that more than 1 million of those people who die will go to hell.[2] Perhaps the number will be more, perhaps less. Nothing in our social science arsenal enables us to measure the true contours of the heart and soul with absolute accuracy; that is God's purview and His alone. But our best research techniques suggest that every day, thousands of people leave this planet for a known and permanently agonizing eternity.

The eternal condemnation and suffering of these million-plus people qualifies as a *bigger tragedy* than the act of dying.

A more devastating aspect of this tragedy is that many of those people were denied an opportunity to learn about the joy and comfort of God's eternal blessings and peace. Nobody—not family members, friends, church members, work associates, educators, public officials, clergy or leisure-time associates—loved them enough to introduce them to the living God. They could have been spared the worst sentence of all had the followers of Christ wholeheartedly shared the good news of salvation through the grace of God with those who were living independent of God's everlasting forgiveness. Millions of the souls that writhe in hell today could have avoided that sentence.

And that is the *biggest tragedy* of all.

# A WARNING FROM LAZARUS

I apparently have a poor memory. The joke around the office is that I write so many books because I can't remember anything. Unfortunately, there is more than a grain of truth in this good-natured ribbing.

My faulty memory strikes in many arenas of my life, including my inability to recall the content of most of the sermons I have heard. Traveling throughout the world and studying and interacting with church leaders have exposed me to some of the best teaching on the planet. Undoubtedly, if I could remember more of the scriptural pearls of wisdom I have heard, I would be a better human being and a more adept servant of Christ.

### A NIGHT AT WILLOW CREEK

Several sermons, however, have attached themselves to my brain tissue. In the early 1980s, my wife and I lived near Chicago and attended Willow Creek Community Church. One winter, our pastor, Bill Hybels, was leading the church through a series on the book of Luke. The series was taught during the midweek service, and I recall arriving at the church one Wednesday evening fatigued from a full day of meetings, negotiations and production. The Chicago winds were typically gusty, the temperature characteristically subzero. We drove eight miles to the church on narrow roads caked with ice, sand and a thin layer of snow. I was not exactly "up" for a night of church, but dutifully I attended.

As Bill read Luke 16:19-31, my comatose mind snapped to attention. His passionate retelling of the story of the rich man banished to hell gripped my heart as few stories ever had. Chills ran down my spine as I heard the plaintive cry of the rich man to Abraham: "I beg you, father, send Lazarus to my father's house, for I have five brothers. Let him warn them, so that they will not also come to this place of torment" (Luke 16:27).

To this day, more than a decade later, I recall that lesson and the horror that filled me as I realized, perhaps for the first time, how horrific a life in hell would be, how significant the death of Christ had been for me and just how imperative it is to use every resource available to share the real truth about life, death, sin and grace with every person I know.

I remember tossing and turning in bed that night, angry that Bill Hybels had so effectively confronted me with the necessity of sharing the gospel with the people I love. I remember thinking about family members who have steadfastly hidden behind denominational allegiance, church attendance and good works, heatedly using these arguments and discounting "that born-again stuff." I remember the emotional pain of realizing that I might be the last hope my family and closest friends have for knowing Jesus in a personal and intimate way. No, in a living, saving way.

As I tried unsuccessfully to rest that night while the wind howled and the moonlight drove shadows across our bedroom, I knew that the rich man who was living in torment forevermore was no different than my friends and family would be unless somebody chose to confront those dear people with God's ways and God's truth.

## An Often Unpopular Role

I did not sleep that night because I knew the "somebody" was meant to be me. It was a role I did not especially want even though God clearly promises that He will bear the burden if I will simply be accessible as the instrument of communication.

The infamous wrestling match between Jacob and God became more real to me that night as I struggled through the mental gymnastics of accepting my responsibilities.[3] Perhaps the turning point came when God revealed to me the irony of the situation: If I could remove my ego long enough to get a clear picture of what was happening, the only people who would really be affected by my decision to share or not to share were the nonbelievers who would miss out on paradise unnecessarily if I remained obstinate.

God used that insight to free me from my insecurities and anxieties about my overt and undeniable inadequacies as an evangelizer. It really doesn't matter if my efforts disappoint me; better to have my ego deflated than to realize that I chose not to enable good people to share eternity with me in God's presence.

# This Book Is About Evangelism

This is a book about evangelism in America as we draw near to the new millennium. It is a book based on what I have learned from a dozen years of research related to America's faith and its ever-changing values and morality. It is *not* a book of theology, doctrine or even statistics.

It is the story of a universal community of faith known as the Church that is called to evangelize but which is slowly removing itself from the evangelical tradition of our forefathers. Instead, the people of God who cumulatively form His family on earth are embracing a culture that wants nothing to do with a God who requires holiness, sacrifice and obedience.

This is a book that describes the current state of affairs and where we may be heading spiritually, as a result of the choices we have made in the past and the choices we seem likely to make today.

■ ■

NONBELIEVERS OFTEN RESPOND TO PEOPLE, GIFTED OR NOT, WHO ARE ACCESSIBLE TO GOD, USED BY GOD AND BLESSED BY GOD THROUGH THE WORKING OF HIS HOLY SPIRIT.

■ ■ ■

### EVANGELISM ALIVE AND WELL

Rest assured, all is not gloom and doom in this tale. In the course of our research, we have uncovered many pockets of exciting evangelistic activity. Yes, millions of Americans' lives *are* being radically and permanently transformed by the grace of God. Many churches and individual believers across the nation *are* having an impact. They are shedding their fears of rejection, are overcoming personal anxieties about the lack of gifts or abilities to adequately represent the God of the universe and are undeterred by the possibility that their words might fall on deaf ears.

These Christians are playing their small but crucial roles in the spiritual drama of the age. They are letting God use them as instruments of grace in a world that eschews such service. These are churches and people who have come to know the unspeakable joy of enabling other human beings to turn away from sin and to choose a relationship with Christ as the cornerstone of their existence. Gifted or not, these are the human beings accessible to God, used by God and blessed by God through the working of His Holy Spirit in their lives and in the lives of the people who hear and respond to the gospel.

In the pages that follow, we will examine the state of Christianity and evangelism in our nation today. This is no small task.

Evangelistic endeavors in America consume billions of dollars and tens of millions of hours every year. Gauging the evangelistic pulse of the nation would require a commitment to understanding the breadth and depth of what is happening through churches, through parachurch ministries and through individual commitments to engage in gospel outreach. No single book can do equal justice to all of the elements related to evangelism in America at the close of the twentieth century. Here are the aspects we will examine:

- Has anyone in this media-saturated, religiously aware nation not heard the gospel? If so, who are they and what will it take to reach them?
- What are the experiences, the objections and the needs of those people who have rejected the church and the Christian faith?
- What people are interested in spreading the Christian faith? What makes them tick, and what are they experiencing in their efforts to further God's kingdom?
- How are evangelizers sharing the Word of God and the message of salvation with nonbelievers? What strategies are working, which are declining, what may work in the future?
- What is the role of evangelism within Christian churches? What novel and effective approaches are churches using to influence the country for Christ?
- What roadblocks are hindering the effective spread of God's Word?
- What will it take to create an evangelistic fervor in America? How can churches and other ministries participate in developing effective and widespread evangelism? What may an individual believer do to maximize his or her determination to be an agent of life transformation by pursuing evangelistic opportunities?

## A YEARNING FOR REVIVAL

If my prayer comes true, this book will not become just another seemingly endless stream of exhortations for you to participate in evangelism because that is God's will for your life. I appreciate and affirm the message of such books.

My purpose is to provide an empirical evaluation of what is and is not happening in evangelism in America today. I long to see revival wash this land of its wayward leanings and evil choices. I desperately want to help expose myths about evangelism and church outreach that stop us from having an impact. I passionately want to encourage the "average" Christian to understand that each of us has a vital part to play in the transformation of our hearts and culture.

For some people, this book may be a needed wake-up call: Get into the game and share the good news, now! For others, it may be a needed wake-up call of another kind: Understand the fields that are ripe for the harvest and act intelligently and strategically, not merely traditionally or routinely. For still others, it may be an affirmation of their diligent and appropriate efforts to serve the living and loving God of creation by living and loving that creation through telling Jesus' remarkable story.

In the process of striving to achieve these ends, I believe you will read some statistics and conclusions that will make you uncomfortable. Having presented some of this information to pastors, church leaders and seminary students, I know how incongruous our actions are with our words, how disappointing the outcomes are, given our hopes, and how disturbing the reality of our world is compared to the dreamworld in which many of us operate.

Today, we share the gospel in a world that has some significant differences from the culture in which Jesus ministered nearly two thousand years ago. We minister in a world that bears limited resemblance to the era of Martin Luther, John Calvin or other renowned defenders of the faith. To be honest, the environment in which we now live is not even like the one in which Billy Graham ministered so powerfully and remarkably just 40 years ago when he burst onto the evangelistic scene.

We cannot be effective if we continue to cling to the old ways, the old strategies, the old assumptions. We do not live in that era, and we cannot be effective if we behave in a manner relevant only to the past.

Does the way we think and act regarding evangelism really matter? I am not trained as a theologian, but my understanding of personal ministry and lifestyle is that one day I will be held accountable by God for everything I have said, done, thought and desired. One line of questioning may relate to my commitment to share the truths about sin and salvation with nonbelievers. I will not be held accountable for other people's decisions regarding the truths and biblical principles I shared with them. But God will take a deep interest in the heart and commitment related to my efforts to introduce other people to His Son.

It also is undeniable that many personal benefits can be realized from reasonable involvement in sharing the good news of Christ's death and resurrection with those who are outside the family of faith. Granted, evangelism done for the purpose of selfish gain neither honors God nor brings us any kind of true reward or satisfaction. But outreach conducted with a heart to serve God and to love His people can be enormously fulfilling.

## A MATTER OF LIFE AND DEATH

Ultimately, this is a book about life and death—true death. You also could say this is a story about your life, your ministry, your purpose. I pray that through this story, we will grow together as partners in reaching a lost, dying, desperately sad and searching world. Although many nonbelievers are unaware of it, the answer to their deepest needs and desires in life is a personal relationship with Jesus Christ.

The challenge to you and to me is to present the truth of the gospel to people in a form they can understand, consider and accept. As we share the truth of salvation, there is no room for compromise, and there is no need to agonize over the outcome if we faithfully play our role and let the Holy Spirit play His part.

We have no time to waste. We cannot know when the end of the human age will arrive, nor when any particular people with whom we have contact will die. Time is of the essence.

**NOTES**
1. Bureau of the Census, *Statistical Abstract of the United States 1994*, prepared by the Department of Commerce in cooperation with the Bureau of the Census (Washington, D.C., 1994).
2. This figure is based on a series of national surveys among random samples of the adult population. In our surveys, we define the term "Christian" for those who say they have made a personal commitment to Jesus Christ that is still important in their lives today, and for those who believe that when they die they will go to heaven because they have confessed their sins and have accepted Jesus Christ as their Savior. This consistently emerges as about 35 percent of the adult population, suggesting that nearly two-thirds of the adult population may be headed for eternal damnation unless they have a change of heart.
3. See Genesis 32:22-32.

# 1

# EVANGELISM IN PERSPECTIVE

If you read many biographies or history books, you will find that people from almost every era of human history have believed they were living in a unique or unusually significant period. From the Bible, you can see this perspective in the words of Moses, David, Solomon, the great prophets of Israel and the apostles John and Paul. Since the days of the Early Church, you can detect this outlook as a shaping influence upon world leaders as varied as Caesar, Luther, Columbus, Napoleon, Washington, Hitler, Kennedy and Mandela.

I believe that America is entering a pivotal moment in its comparatively brief history. We are experiencing the convergence of two significant crises: cultural and spiritual. Without a doubt, these crises are intimately related. In all likelihood, when one of these crises is resolved, the fate of the other will be determined as well. The way we resolve these challenges to our nation's character and security will complete the redefinition of the United States that began some 30 years ago.[1]

The heart of the cultural crisis is the struggle to determine the values of the nation. It seems that the defining element in the process of reconfiguring the culture has been a progressive movement to reconceptualize moral truth. The result has been that we now define what is "right" and what is "wrong" quite differently than ever before. This new view of morality, ethics and the role and character of humankind has reshaped personal relationships, marketplace activity and personal perspectives regarding the meaning and purpose in life.[2]

## A CULTURE IN CRISIS

This recasting of our most fundamental moral and ethical views has occurred because of a concurrent shift in the nation's spiritual climate and outlook. Historically, the Bible has served as our touchstone for determining what is appropriate and inappropriate.

In recent years, however, it has become fashionable to regard the Bible as a document of antiquity, a Book that unwisely has been revered as a reference manual for those in search of guidance regarding lifestyles and values. In the present "politically correct" era, distinguished by a virulent championing of moral relativism and the fierce defense of radical individualism, pluralism and all manner of diversity, spirituality relates more to the discovery and healing of self than to the discovery of and intimacy with a supreme being. To paraphrase a well-worn expression from the cartoon character Pogo, "We have met the deity and He is us."

Normally, a cultural crisis of this nature would be influenced by the moral underpinnings derived from the spiritual passion and commitment of the nation. Whether intentional or not, however, those people who initiated redirection of our cultural mores, traditions and truths tied the values revolution to a renewed vision of faith and religion. Consequently, America's cultural changes have spun out of control because of an absence of a stable, reliable moral center to act as the anchor to which every significant transition is tied.

Some analysts have concluded wrongly that the problem is a changing America. Quite the contrary is true; if America were *not* experiencing some form of change, it would die. Change is a natural and unstoppable process in every culture; it is a constant process of renewal and development. But change may have positive or negative effects. All change is not created equal. Cultures that have developed to a higher level of individual fulfillment, humanitarian behavior and spiritual maturity have relied upon the moral foundation of the culture as a purifier through which every change is filtered.

For many decades, America prospered in the midst of considerable social change because it was rooted to a moral base that served as the heart of the culture. During the first half of this century, for instance, we survived suffrage, prohibition, two world wars, a stock-market crash, religious scandals, technological breakthroughs and national health epidemics because of our ability to lean on the moral core that defined the national personality and perspective. Without the consistent and dependable spiritual base that defined our morals, values, lifestyles and dreams, today's cultural turbulence would have arrived much sooner.

## THE AMERICAN EXPERIMENT AT RISK

Today, the viability of the bold American experiment in freedom, democracy and liberty is in jeopardy. It was the moral base supporting our systems of government and commerce that enabled the United States to rise above the numerous failed and flawed societal approaches that have been introduced, tested and abandoned throughout the world since the time of Jesus Christ. Many intelligent, well-intentioned and articulate people somehow miss this insight. They relegate religious affairs to the realm of the emotional and illogical, asserting that religious views are an intrusion into our freedom and privacy, instead of rightly perceiving them to be the very basis of the lifestyle we cherish so dearly. The sociopolitical transformation they seek to spark cannot achieve the lasting, positive influence they desire simply because it lacks the heart of a revolution (i.e., a moral base drawn from spiritual truth).

■ ■

## EVERY REVIVAL IN THE HISTORY OF THE MODERN WORLD HAS BEEN GROUNDED IN AN EXPLOSION OF PRAYER AND EVANGELISM.

■ ■ ■

During this past quarter century or so, Christianity in America has withstood a powerful challenge to its strength and supremacy as the basis of its law, order, virtue and purpose. The Christian Church in this country continues to be rocked by the social forces aligned against it.

The results of the relentless battle to destroy the centrality of Christianity are evident: media mockery of Christians and their faith, declining church attendance, a shrinking pool of people who are ardently committed to their faith, history books and political debates that eliminate or deny the positive influence of Christianity, the reduction of religious liberties (ironically conducted in the name of religious freedom), a diverted national focus away from the things of God to the vices and pleasures of humankind, the waning influence of religious institutions and spokespersons, and severe "legal" restrictions against the application of the Christian faith to all dimensions of life.

## A TIME FOR REVIVAL

Our present circumstance is not unprecedented in human history. A comforting realization is that historically, conditions often reach their nadir just before the dawning of a period of awakening or enlightenment. Often matters must become so deplorable that not even those who helped to engineer such circumstances maintain an interest in continuing the course they charted.

The result is a rapid transformation from decadence to repentance and cultural renewal. From a Christian perspective, we are immersed in a bruising but exciting time because the social and moral conditions are right for spiritual revival.

Students of church history and contemporary culture will immediately see the problem with the proposition that America is on the precipice of revival. Every revival in the history of the modern world has been grounded in an explosion of prayer and evangelism.

In the time directly preceding an outbreak of spiritual revival, churches focus their energy and resources on congregational repentance, personal commitment to outreach, and preparation for the potential outpouring of God's Holy Spirit upon the land and the influx of new converts. The hole in the hypothesis that America is living on the edge of revival is that as matters stand today, the Church is ill-poised to initiate and to sustain a revolution of the human heart and soul.

No one can deny, however, that our present cultural and spiritual conditions are ripe for a massive return to God by the people of America. Today, approximately 262 million people live in the United States. By my calculations, based on large-scale surveys of the population, 187 million of those people have yet to accept Jesus Christ as their Lord and Savior.

The non-Christian segment of the national population is so extensive that if it were a nation, it would constitute the fifth most populated nation on planet earth.[3] Our surveys consistently detect a large (and growing) majority of adults who are dissatisfied and are searching for something more meaningful to live for than bigger homes, fatter paychecks, trimmer bodies, more erotic affairs and extended leisure time. Tens of millions of Americans are open to a set of spiritual truths that will set them free from the shackles of worldliness.[4]

## WHERE IS THE WORD?

Our research also shows that evangelism is not the revitalizing factor many Christians wish it were. How ironic that during this period of swelling need for the proclamation of the gospel and the healing powers of the Church, the ranks of the messengers have dissipated to anemic proportions.

Why does this paradox exist (i.e., the growing need for God's love and truth in a culture where the Church seems less emphatic about communicating and demonstrating that love)? I believe it largely has to do with our misperception of circumstances and misinterpretation of responsibilities. For example:

- Most Christians believe (incorrectly) that evangelism is meant to happen primarily during the Sunday morning worship. Amazingly, just one-third of all adults contend that they personally have any responsibility or obligation to share their religious views with other people.

Most people are content to let the Church do the work of spreading the religious party line. Consequently, as long as numerous churches are accessible to the populace, Christians tend to feel secure that evangelism is happening or, at least, has the ability to happen. The fact that we have about 320,000 Protestant and Catholic churches in the United States has seduced the Christian community into complacency regarding the necessity of enthusiastic, multifaceted, aggressive evangelism outside of church services.

- Americans major on categorizing and pigeonholing everything. Compartmentalizing reality has become one of our chief defenses against an increasingly complex and stressful existence; mentally ordering our world into well-defined niches is one way we make a complicated world more simple and manageable. Sadly, we have included our religious faith in this reductionist life perspective.

In our well-intentioned but ultimately harmful simplification of Christian experience and responsibility, we have become accustomed to thinking of evangelism as the exclusive domain of three types of people: pastors, missionaries and people who have the spiritual gift of evangelism. We have perhaps 800,000 ordained or full-time, church-based ministers, about 50,000 missionaries and an undetermined number of people who possess the spiritual gift of evangelism (our best estimate is perhaps 2 million or 3 million people who would assert that they have been given this special ability).[5]

Even if we exaggerate the numbers (that is, if we speak "evangelastically"), we still could not honestly claim the existence of a pool of more than 5 million of these alleged outreach specialists. That leaves an enormous majority of Christians who feel mentally and emotionally freed from the concern and responsibility for ongoing evangelistic efforts.

- Fund-raising and marketing efforts by national parachurch ministries have created a sense that the evangelism professionals are on the job, are in control, are achieving success and are able to handle the task of reaching those who have escaped the net and remain unreached.

Televangelists commonly speak of the "tens of thousands" of people who have accepted Christ as a result of their ministry or the "millions" who are exposed to the gospel as a result of their broadcasting and related efforts. Letters, events and telemarketing messages designed by parachurch ministries to raise funds frequently mention the dramatic and enormous evangelistic effect the organization is having around the globe.

Although such claims may hype the donor base to give more money, it simultaneously reduces the person's perceived need to be an active participant in evangelizing the world, other than through emptying his or her wallet so that the professional ministers may continue their harvest.

- In today's information-rich, values-poor culture in which success means comfort and truth means popularity, many committed Christians have been led to believe that it is unthinkable that God would allow His people to share valuable information and would then experience rejection. Would a loving God subject His own servants to such disgrace and dishonor?[6]

Given that more than 80 million adults contend that being on the receiving end of an evangelistic pitch is "annoying" and knowing that several million born-again Christians refuse to describe themselves as born again for fear of becoming social outcasts, many churches and Christians have chosen to "soft sell" the gospel.[7] The result has been a rise in keeping religion private. Increasingly, Christians and non-Christians alike opt for a nation in which people are free to practice their religion as long as it is done in secret (or quietly).

Public outbursts of religiosity, whether through public prayer, exhortations to operate with biblical values and principles, or interpersonal proselytizing, are looked upon as evidence of inappropriate and crude behavior. In this environment, a "real Christian" is defined as a person who is compassionate enough to keep his or her beliefs private.

And so the world's greatest gift is now faced with becoming the world's greatest secret. Many of the people whom Christ is counting on to spread the light of salvation throughout a spiritually darkened nation have largely succumbed to pressures from the target population itself to maintain a reverent silence about a matter as personal as spiritual beliefs.

Rather than commit to the hardships associated with being influence agents, they have become influenced agents—influenced by the very society they have been called to transform with the love of Christ, for the glory of God and the benefit of those who would be transformed.

## FOR SUCH A TIME AS THIS

I do not buy some of the current arguments that the real problem is now sophisticated Americans are or how different our culture is from that in which Jesus ministered. If you examine some of the hallmark characteristics of both cultures, it is curious how similar the cultures of America 1995 and Palestine A.D. 30 are. They may have more in common than in contrast.

Consider some of the cultural and spiritual parallels of the two cultures:

- The political system is characterized by widespread corruption, public distrust of political leaders and extreme egotism among those people in positions of authority.
- The government places a heavy tax burden on the people; the people regularly complain about the excessive taxation powers of government.
- Christians who attempt to influence the prevailing government in light of their religious beliefs are ignored, ridiculed or persecuted.
- Most people think of themselves as religious. However, the religious practices of the day are characterized by legalism, idolatry and doctrinal syncretism.
- The population is ethnically diverse, speaks various languages and exhibits a broad spectrum of lifestyles and customs.
- Poverty is widespread. Many people lack housing, food, health care and employment.
- Miraculous events and healings are looked upon with great skepticism by the general population.
- Most people look to the state to provide for their ultimate fulfillment and comfort; their idea of happiness and salvation is God providing some type of sociopolitical solution.
- A majority believe that God's favor may be won by a person's performing a sufficient quality and quantity of good deeds.
- Though there are moments of peace, the people live with the constant threat of war and with a constant (and expensive) military presence.
- Productive employment is expected of every able-bodied male, but taking advantage of leisure opportunities is also a top priority.
- Sexual promiscuity is common.
- The workplace is filled with entrepreneurs who work from their homes or small shops in the marketplace.
- The judicial system is slow and unpredictable and the court dockets are crowded. The vast majority of prisoners are male.
- A high degree of household transience is in existence, resulting in difficulties in establishing a sense of community.
- Most men and women are married at some time in young adulthood. Most married couples produce children.
- Education is a means to economic ascendancy. However, most

people do not take full advantage of the educational opportunities available to them, choosing to enter the workplace instead.

- Most adults adopt the religion of their parents.
- Christians are deemed to be intolerant, given their espousal of the "one true faith" and their belief in moral absolutes.
- Human achievement is seen as the pathway to earthly success and immortality. Reliance upon spiritual truth as the means to success and fulfillment is viewed as ignorance, as irrelevant and as a sign of weakness.[8]

Just as Jesus' coming some two thousand years ago was no accident, we must also understand that His example (and that of the apostles) is a perfectly adaptable model for us to institute today.

■ ■

# THE EVANGELIZER PLAYS A ROLE IN THE CONVERSION PROCESS BUT WILL NOT BE HELD ACCOUNTABLE FOR THE CHOICE MADE BY THOSE WHO HEAR THE GOSPEL.

■ ■ ■

Obviously, our society differs significantly from that of first-century Palestine in many ways. Even so, like the residents of the Roman Empire two millennia ago, our culture is well-positioned for the message of hope that Jesus commanded us to share in bold and unapologetic ways.

The apostle Paul, the world's first great itinerant evangelist, provided us with the cornerstone principle, drawn from the example of Jesus' ministry, for effectively communicating the gospel. Paul admonished the believers in the church of Corinth to contextualize the message—that is, to share the gospel with a culture so that it could be understood without compromising or reshaping the work of Christ (1 Cor. 9:19-23). The apostle understood that he was called to be a faithful messenger of a timeless message and that the message itself would be relevant to all people in all walks of life, knowing that the manner in which the information was proclaimed might have to shift from one cultural context to another.

## EVANGELISTIC TRUTHS STILL APPLY

Consider some of the central tenets of evangelism prepared for us in the Bible. These principles are every bit as dynamic and pertinent to us as they were to Peter, John, Matthew, James and the rest of the ragtag army who followed Jesus and then turned their world upside down by retelling His story.

√ The message is God's. The means of getting the message to those who need to hear it is by people communicating that message through words and actions that are consistent with the lessons in the Bible.

√ God can, has and will use anybody who is open to serving Him to convey the gospel. He will bless the efforts of His servants whether they are gifted as evangelizers or not.

√ We are called to take advantage of opportunities to share our faith in Christ and to make the most of those opportunities. However, the act of converting a person from condemned sinner to forgiven and loved disciple of Christ is the job of the Holy Spirit. The evangelizer plays a role in the conversion process but will not be held accountable for the choice made by those who hear the gospel.

√ The most powerful attraction to a nonbeliever is seeing the life of someone transformed by the reality of the gospel. Although a verbal explanation of that faith is helpful toward facilitating a nonbeliever's decision to follow Christ, a verbal proclamation without a lifestyle that supports that proclamation is powerless.

√ The most effective evangelists are the most obedient and committed Christians. They need not have formal theological training, a full-time position in a church or credentials such as ordination. They need a passion for Christ, a desire to make Him known to the world and the willingness to be used in any and all situations to help usher others into the kingdom of God.

√ Evangelism is the bridge we build between our love for God and our love for other people. Through the work of the Holy Spirit, through us, God can complete His transformation of a person for His purposes and glory.

√ We cannot give away what we don't have. Therefore, we must be in close relationship with God and must be open to being used by Him as a conduit of His grace.

√ Effective outreach always involves sincere and fervent prayer that God will bless those efforts, although there is no guarantee of the nonbeliever making the right choice.

√ Knowing, trusting and using God's Word is central to leading a person to a lifesaving faith in Jesus.

√ When we intelligently share our faith with nonbelievers, it pleases God.

√ Every Christian must be ready at all times and in all situations to share his or her faith in Christ with those who do not have a relationship with Christ.

√ Evangelism is not meant to be limited by human convenience or preference. It is to be done with obedience and faith.

√ The most effective evangelistic efforts are those that are simple and sincere.

√ Evangelism that starts at the nonbeliever's point of felt need and ties the gospel into that area of need has the greatest capacity for capturing the mind and heart of the non-Christian.

√ Outreach efforts that take advantage of the credibility, accessibility and trust of an existing friendship have a better chance of succeeding than does "cold call" evangelism. However, God uses all sincere and appropriate attempts to serve Him and to love others by sharing the gospel.[9]

There can be no denying—though some people have tried—that you and I, as fellow believers in Jesus Christ, have a responsibility to share the good news of this free gift of ultimate love with the rest of God's creation. The motivation must not be whether people are anxious to hear the gospel, but whether we have been called to deliver that message to the unbelieving world.

## THE HARSH SIDE OF SUCCESS

Of course, history also shows us that Christian evangelism is not always enthusiastically received. All but one of the apostles were martyred. In fact, since the crucifixion of Christ, it is estimated that more than 40 million believers have been slain because they have promoted or defended their Christian faith.[10]

This raises an important question for you and me: Why have so many people willingly sacrificed life on earth for physical death, a death oftentimes cruel and torturous? The answer, I believe, lies in the depth of their understanding of what Christianity is all about.

In America today, as in many nations around the globe for centuries, success has been defined in earthly, material ways: comfort, longevity, popularity, emotional peace, intelligence, freedom and financial independence. Increasingly, we see our country turning to the notion that it takes a combination of these conditions to achieve real success, which sometimes are mistakenly labeled as "happiness."

In heaven today, success is defined the same way as it was defined two thousand years ago by Jesus Christ during His earthly ministry, or thousands of years before that as God revealed His will to Israel. *Success is faithfulness and obedience to God.* Everything else is a diversion. In the end, all that matters is whether we have given God control of our lives and been faithful to Him.

As we strive to understand what faithfulness means, the Bible is our best and most authoritative source to study. Obedience is defined as:

- A personal commitment to Christ in which we acknowledge Him to be our one and only Savior (see John 3:16-18).
- A personal commitment to holiness, perhaps best defined by Paul as the fruit of the Spirit (see Gal. 5:22-24; 1 Thess. 4:7).
- A personal commitment to pleasing God, not for the purposes of salvation, but as a way of bringing Him glory, honor and pleasure through our obedience to His commands (see Exod. 20:1-21; Rom. 12:1,2).
- A personal commitment to consistent worship of God alone (see Matt. 4:10).
- A personal commitment to performing selfless acts of service for others, motivated by the exemplary love of Christ and conducted to reflect our love for God and His creation (see John 13:1-17).
- A personal commitment to share the good news of Christ's sacrificial life, death and resurrection (see Matt. 28:19).

Why have 40 million people been martyred since the death of Christ? Because at least 40 million people had their faith radically challenged and they refused to back down from following Christ no matter what the cost of that relationship. To those saints, the very purpose of life was wrapped up in their understanding of the fullness of the Christian life.

These martyrs viewed their relationship with Jesus Christ as one worth dying for. Their faith was more than a simple series of religious truths that enabled them to gain earthly riches, to be seen in the right places at the right times or to gain new insights into human character. Their faith was the defining thread of their lives. Their refusal to renounce their faith, even at the cost of their lives, dramatically illustrates how they defined success and purpose in life.

What do these martyrs' examples say to those of us in a different milieu, where people may be ridiculed for their public commitment to Christianity but certainly not threatened with physical death for their commitment to Jesus Christ? Their examples represent nothing less than a standard for comparison of how deeply committed we must be to Christ, of how passionate we are to be about our faith and of how completely we are willing to trust in the promises of God.

Do you buy the notion, beyond a morsel of doubt, that "in all things God works for the good of those who love him, who have been called according to his purpose" (Rom. 8:28)? Do you truly believe that His grace is sufficient for you (2 Cor. 12:9)? Do you really accept the idea that the greatest end of humankind is to "love the Lord your God with all your heart and with all your soul and with all your mind" (Matt. 22:37, also see v. 38)?

## EVANGELISM IN PERSPECTIVE

Evangelism, then, is one of the most important elements of being faithful and obedient to God. But it is not the only aspect that makes us valued servants of the Father. Some people may consider this as heresy, but I suggest that evangelism may not be the single most important activity in life.

Evangelism is critically important, but so are other elements of the Christian life. Christianity that focuses exclusively on evangelism and ignores the other critical factors of faithfulness is a dangerous, imbalanced Christianity. A life of devotion to Christ that does not include a focus upon evangelism is similarly imbalanced.

The measure of emphasis we individually place upon evangelism depends upon many elements: the opportunities we have, our ability to communicate clearly, our maturity as believers, the spiritual gifts and special talents God provides and so forth. Balance, then, does not necessarily mean that you and I have to spend an equal amount of time on evangelistic efforts as, for example, in discipling, serving, praying and worshiping.

As a useful analogy, I think about the meaning of chemical balance in a swimming pool. Could you imagine swimming in a pool comprised of equal amounts of water, chlorine, acid, ash and each of the other key chemicals? Jump into such a concoction and you would have a memorably painful swim! The chemicals must be balanced in a way that creates a viable environment.

In the same way, leading a truly balanced Christian life requires that we understand ourselves and our calling and be true to both. As we share our faith with others, we must ensure that evangelism is coming from a heart that wants to engage in it as an act of love toward God and service to humanity, and that it is done in the context of our efforts to be complete and diligent agents of God.

## THE QUESTION OF RELEVANCE

Some people ask if evangelism is still relevant today. The question does not so much inquire about the utility of sharing the gospel as it questions the validity of the Christian faith for an age that is more complex and perhaps more perverse than any previous one. The question alludes to a crisis of faith rather than to a true concern about the value of exhorting others to follow Christ.

The fact that many Christians even raise such a question, however, points out the importance of dogged commitment to balanced Christianity. People must hear the gospel proclaimed. They must study the foundations of the faith. They must see the faith modeled in the lives of other believers. And they must pursue maturing in their faith through constant devotion to spiritual growth.

Evangelism is relevant only as long as the Christian faith is relevant to the people of the earth. Toward that end, I suggest that, if properly understood and explained, the gospel is equally relevant in all ages and perhaps is needed more now than ever given the conscious depravity of our culture.

The message of God's love for His creation is more relevant than the messages communicated in today's most popular songs and movies, more relevant than the major political issues that are being debated so hotly on Capitol Hill and more relevant than many of the decisions that seem like life-or-death choices at our places of work. The task that you and I have is to think and pray about how God might use us most effectively and significantly in spreading the good news.

Whether a need exists today for evangelism is not really the issue. Whether we will be committed to a continual and relevant presentation of the gospel to those who are not followers of Christ is the real challenge for us to accept.

## NOTES

1. For a further discussion of the spiritual and cultural crises facing America, see George Barna, *Virtual America* (Ventura, Calif.: Regal Books, 1994), chaps. 9 and 10; and George Barna, *If Things Are So Good, Why Do I Feel So Bad?* (Chicago: Moody Press, 1994).
2. Ibid.
3. These figures are based on data from our national studies, which indicate that about 35 percent of the adult population is Christian, plus 10 percent of the population under 18. The only nations that have a larger population base than non-Christian America are China, India, Indonesia and Russia.
4. Such spiritual disaffection and searching is evident in a number of books. Some books you might consult include George Barna's *Virtual America; If Things Are So Good, Why Do I Feel So Bad?* and *Absolute Confusion* (Ventura, Calif.: Regal Books, 1993); Russell Chandler, *Racing Toward 2001* (Grand Rapids, Mich.: Zondervan Publishing House, 1992); Os Guinness, *The American Hour* (New York: Free Press, 1993); James Hunter, *Culture Wars* (New York: Basic Books, 1993).

5. These projections are based on data reported in Kenneth Bedell, ed., *The Yearbook of American and Canadian Churches 1994* (Nashville: Abingdon Press, 1994); Bryant Myers, *The Changing Shape of World Missions* (Monrovia, Calif.: MARC, 1994); and national studies conducted by the Barna Research Group, Ltd.

6. In this politically correct world, even the questions get distorted. The appropriate question is not whether God would "subject" His people to harm; the answer to that question is no. However, if the question is whether God would call upon His people to be His ambassadors in situations in which they might encounter physical danger or harm, the answer is yes. If you doubt this, study the life of the apostle Paul or read Paul's personal description of what he encountered in his quest to be faithful to God's call (see 2 Cor. 11:23-29).

7. Research on how many people consider evangelism to be annoying is described in *Absolute Confusion* on pp. 124 and 168. Insights regarding how many born-again Christians call themselves by this label and how many refuse to be known by this term is from the report "Born Again" by George Barna (Glendale, Calif.: Barna Research Group, Ltd., 1991). Please do not misinterpret the reference to churches that "soft sell" the gospel as a veiled allusion to seeker churches, megachurches or churches engaging in a contemporary style of ministry. I am referring to churches that facilitate "cheap grace" or that fail to provide a strong and honest presentation of the gospel. Many of the leading seeker, mega- and contemporary-style churches do not hold back when it comes to challenging visitors to accept the gospel.

8. Church historians provide a useful understanding of the cultural context in which Jesus ministered; a plethora of contemporary writers focus upon the modern context. Among the sources that helped me understand Jesus' cultural milieu were H. Richard Niebuhr, *Christ and Culture* (New York: HarperCollins, 1951); Robert Clouse, Richard Pierard and Edwin Yamauchi, *Two Kingdoms* (Chicago: Moody Press, 1993); and Gordon Moyes, *Discovering Jesus* (Sutherland, NSW, Australia: Albatross Books, 1984).

9. Many leaders have written insightfully about the elements that make evangelism appropriate and effective. Among the resources that have been most useful to me have been Robert Coleman, *The Master Plan of Evangelism* (Grand Rapids, Mich.: Fleming H. Revell Company, 1963); Dick Innes, *I Hate Witnessing* (Ventura, Calif.: Regal Books, 1983); Ron Sider, *One-Sided Christianity?* (Grand Rapids, Mich.: Zondervan Publishing House, 1993); and George Hunter, *How to Reach Secular People* (Nashville: Abingdon Press, 1992).

10. This estimate is from research by David Barrett and Todd Johnson, which was reported in their book, *Our Globe and How to Reach It* (Birmingham, Ala.: New Hope, 1990).

# 2

# IS AMERICA
# SATURATED WITH
# THE GOSPEL?

Is America drowning in a sea of competing gospel messages?

Has any adult in America really not heard the gospel?

To many evangelicals, asking these questions sounds like heresy.[1] Every time I pose these possibilities to a gathering of evangelical pastors, there is a palpable change in the room temperature. The surroundings turn decidedly chilly with alarming rapidity. Yet, unless we can realistically face and answer such queries, it is difficult to sustain the energy and resources needed to continue effective evangelism in a culture that is generally opposed to overt religious posturing and proselytizing.

## REACHING EVERY HOME

Despite an environment in which public preaching and promotion of the gospel is widely criticized, thousands of Christian ministries have resolved not to rest until the United States has been saturated with the core message of the Bible.

Driven by the realization that Christ will not return until the entire world has been confronted with the gospel and by the related awareness that those who do not hear and accept God's offer of eternal salvation will suffer eternally, enormous effort is devoted to saturation evangelism.

### THE MEANS ARE FAMILIAR

In recent years, the thrust among many has been to "reach every home for Christ." This has taken innumerable forms, some of which may be familiar:

- Extensive broadcasting of gospel messages on television, through event-related programs aired by independent evangelistic ministries such as the Billy Graham Evangelistic Association; through religious networks such as Trinity Broadcasting or The Inspirational Network; and by weekly broadcasts of church services and Bible-teaching programs. More than $200 million is spent every year by evangelistic ministries on airtime.

- The radio waves are filled with preaching and teaching programs, many of which are purportedly designed to appeal to the needs and interests of nonbelievers. More than $100 million is spent by radio ministries in their attempts to reach nonbelievers.

- Several organizations have developed extensive projects meant to reach every home with the gospel. Campus Crusade for Christ, for instance, has launched citywide campaigns in which churches cooperatively are assigned sections of the city and send church members to homes, offer non-Christian homeowners a free video of the full-length, evangelistic film *Jesus* and return some days later for a postviewing discussion of the experience. Other organizations are dedicated to reaching homes through other media, such as getting gospel literature into the hands of every adult in a target area either through mailings, in-person contact or events, or by telephoning every household in a community and discussing religious matters with them.

- Some denominations and independent churches have concluded that starting new churches is an effective means of reaching non-Christian people. It is estimated that between the years 1990 and 2000, goals have been and will be made to open more than 40,000 new churches in America, ostensibly as a means of reaching every person in the nation with the gospel.

- More than 5,000 nonchurch organizations whose primary purpose is evangelism within America are sanctioned by the Internal Revenue Service to receive tax deductible donations. These run the gamut from literature distribution entities (e.g., American Tract League, ACTS International, American Bible Society, Good News Publishers and other publishers, which cumulatively distribute more than 100 million tracts every year!) to high school ministries (e.g., Youth for Christ, Young Life) to social service centers (e.g., Salvation Army outposts, the International Union of Gospel Missions, which are center-city rescue missions located in large cities nationwide) to more than 2,000 itinerant evangelists who travel frequently, making public presentations of the gospel to crowds ranging from packed stadiums to a handful of businessmen meeting for lunch.

- Home media that are evangelistic in nature are also a prime indus-try these days. For instance, several hundred books devoted to evangelism—either preparing Christians for more effective out-reach or encouraging non-Christians to follow Christ—are pub-lished each year. Christian music—predominantly traditional gospel or contemporary Christian music—also promotes the mes-sage of Christ on tape, CD, video and laser disc (and gets airplay on the radio). The aggregate revenues from Christian books and music exceeds $1 billion every year. As much as 10 percent of that total may be associated with products that are purely evangelistic.

Little doubt remains that Americans are bombarded with opportunities to hear or to see the gospel in one form or another. The advent of new tech-nologies promotes additional alternatives for reaching the masses, including on-line bulletin-board services related to Christian inquiry and dialogue and CD-ROM discs related to Christian apologetics.

In this age of information, the Christian evangelistic message may not receive the prolific exposure achieved by nonreligious messages, but the evangelistic theme is undeniably present in the marketplace at all times.

## BOMBING ON THE BASICS

But we have learned that *being exposed to information does not mean that peo-ple absorb it, understand it or embrace it.*

For instance, if I told you that 9 out of 10 American adults cannot accu-rately define the meaning of the "Great Commission," you might laugh at such a preposterous notion. If I then said that nearly 7 out of 10 American adults have no clue what the term "John 3:16" means or that barely one-third of all adults know the meaning of the expression "the gospel," you probably would question my understanding of American culture.

Amazingly, however, our research has shown that these statistics are on the mark. Most Americans may have heard key phrases or principles from the Bible, but if they are able to recall those expressions, they remain baf-fled about what those terms mean. As a nation, our understanding of God, Jesus Christ, the Christian faith, the Bible and critical concepts such as sal-vation by grace are a mile wide and an inch deep.[2]

The Great Commission, Jesus' charge to His followers found in Matthew 28:19,20, is nearly 2,000 years old. It is one of the defining commands of Jesus, given as a core challenge to all of His followers, and a central element in the stated mission of churches, denominations and parachurch organi-zations worldwide.

But the typical American adult, who has undoubtedly been exposed to this long-standing challenge many times, has no recollection of the content of the challenge. We discovered that when asked outright to define the meaning of the term, 9 out of 10 adults (86 percent) admitted that they did not know—they did not even hazard a guess. Another 5 percent offered an incorrect answer. Just 9 percent of all Americans correctly described the Great Commission.

John 3:16 is probably the most often-cited Scripture verse relating to salvation. You can see the citation on signs displayed at football games and on highway billboards. It is a staple in the messages preached on TV and in evangelistic crusades. It is a verse memorized by thousands of young children who attend Sunday School classes at their churches.

■ ■

### MORE ADULTS ARE CAPABLE OF ACCURATELY NAMING THE TOP-RATED PRIME-TIME TELEVISION SHOWS...THAN ARE ABLE TO ACCURATELY STATE THE DEFINING THEME OF THE CHRISTIAN FAITH.

■ ■ ■

In spite of the wide promotion received by this dynamic verse, 2 out of every 3 adults said they did not know what John 3:16 says and would not offer a guess. Another 1 out of 10 adults tried to recall the verse but provided descriptions that were not close. This means that 75 percent of the nation either could not guess or guessed inaccurately.

As a nation founded on Christian principles, settled by people who sought religious freedom, and in a nation where church attendance is comparatively high and the Bible remains the best-selling book of all time, you would expect a pivotal term such as "the gospel" to have near-universal recognition.

Once again, however, our lack of knowledge of even the most basic biblical elements is astounding. One-third of the nation has no idea what the term "the gospel" refers to (31 percent). Another one-third tried to define the term but did so inaccurately (32 percent). Among the remaining one-third, half described the gospel as the good news of Jesus' death and resurrection undertaken to save people from their sins.

The remaining group provided the more generic response that the gospel refers to the first four books of the New Testament. (This latter response is not technically correct, of course, but was close enough to motivate us to be charitable in our assessments.)

How many Americans are able to correctly describe the meaning of all three of these fundamental terms: the gospel, John 3:16 and the Great

Commission? Just *4 percent*. Put that into context. More adults are capable of accurately naming the top-rated prime-time television shows, of identifying the names of the lead characters in fictional movies such as *The Godfather* or TV series such as *The Three Stooges* and of accurately recalling the advertising slogans of American Express or United Airlines than are able to accurately state the defining theme of the Christian faith.

It might interest you to know that people who have chosen to commit their lives to Christ, the segment of the population I will refer to as "born-again Christians," do not fare much better when it comes to defining these phrases.[3] Only 2 out of every 10 (19 percent) knew the meaning of the Great Commission. Half correctly described the content of John 3:16, and 6 out of 10 knew the meaning of the term "the gospel."

These proportions amount to something less than a ringing endorsement of the depth of knowledge of the central principles and truths of the Christian faith among those who are the most avid adherents of the faith.

## A PARADOX TO PONDER

Here's another paradox to consider. How many people do you encounter who reflect a "Christian" lifestyle, values system or countenance? Most adults claim they know of very few people, if any, whose lives are clearly transformed or consistently guided by their religious faith. At the same time, we also know that 9 out of 10 Americans (88 percent) label themselves as "Christian."

How is it possible that most adults think of themselves as Christian yet struggle to identify anyone they know whose life is shaped by his or her Christian leanings? It is largely because we have become a nation separated into three "classes" of Christians.

The smallest of the three segments consisted of those people who are true devotees of Christ. They have not only turned to Him as their only means of salvation but their lives are clearly different from before they committed themselves to Him, and they are intentionally and continually maturing in their faith.

The second group, which is somewhat larger, are people who are born again but who have never grown much beyond their basic commitment to Christ. They have the assurance of eternal salvation, but they have failed to become true disciples of the Master. Instead, they have been content to follow religious routines and to do what they must to get by. Though they have the opportunity of knowing God in the deepest possible way, they have chosen to take the easy route rather than to work diligently to perfect their faith. The dominant group members are "cultural Christians."

As for the third class, millions of Americans attend churches that promote Christian doctrine but do not translate that doctrine into a personal commitment to Christ or a changed lifestyle. Millions more simply define themselves as Christian because they are American and they perceive the national religious character to be generally "Christian." To these people, you are automatically a Christian until you consciously choose to declare yourself to be something else. From a biblical point of view, the multitudes in this segment are not Christians; they are self-deceived, unregenerate people who have placed their trust in the wrong things.

Adults in all three of these groups have heard sermons about biblical spirituality, have participated in programs related to orthodox Christianity and probably have been in classes (Sunday School, small groups) that explained the doctrine of salvation by grace. But most of those adults in the cultural Christian camp have yet to make a true profession of faith in Christ.

### IMMUNE TO THE GOSPEL

Undoubtedly, one of the rudest awakenings I have ever received in my efforts to help churches grow was the discovery born from our research a few years ago that *half of all adults who attend Protestant churches on a typical Sunday morning are not Christian!*[4] For several years, I had been analyzing data with the assumption that if a person were in church, the chances were better than even that the person had the foundation of true faith in Christ in place.

For years, I had been lulled into the comforting but erroneous notion that every Sunday morning I was singing praises to God along with the convinced. Little did I realize that a huge portion of those in churches across the land—yes, even those sitting in my church, in *my* pew, in *my* Sunday School class—were nonbelievers. Perhaps I had been lured into such an assumption by their own sense of peace about their spiritual standing. Indeed, most of these people think of themselves as believers who are on the "safe" side of God's judgment.

Disturbed by this knowledge, we conducted additional research among the non-Christians who regularly attended churches. The purpose of the research was to determine how someone could go to worship and teaching services, week after week, and emerge from the experience apparently no closer to really knowing Christ than they had been before. The result of our explorations was frightening: Rather than introducing people to Christ, churches had effectively *anesthetized* these regulars to the gospel.

These religious folk had been exposed to the gospel in such a predictable, repetitious manner so many times, some of them starting from the time they first crawled in the church nursery, that they could recite the words backward and forward. But in spite of their familiarity with the phrasing, the behaviors and the church governmental structure, they lived without having a shred of insight into what a relationship with Christ was all about.

And the problem is not that these church attenders are newcomers. We would raise a shout of praise if they were spiritually searching people who finally chose to give God a chance to show what He has to offer. Unfortunately, we also discerned that the typical person who attends church regularly and does not know Jesus in a personal, life-changing way has been attending church for an average of 10 years or longer! This seems incredible, but it is true.

Through subsequent research, we have learned that those people who sit in church and know the routine but are not truly integrated into God's kingdom have embraced many of the right doctrines and beliefs. For instance, they believe that God is the omnipotent Creator of the universe, they believe in the Trinity, they accept the fact that Jesus was human, that the Holy Spirit lives in believers, that Mary was a virgin when she conceived Jesus, that the miracles described in the Bible all happened, that forgiveness of sins is possible only through Jesus Christ and that prayer has the power to change lives and circumstances. Yet, in spite of many accurate perspectives on the material and spiritual worlds, these people have yet to understand what a real relationship with Jesus Christ means.

Look around you the next time you are at your church to worship God. Chances are that a significant number of the friends and acquaintances in your congregation have never committed their lives to Christ. Do they acknowledge His earthly existence, His death and resurrection, His heavenly presence today, His ability to forgive sins and His unique standing as the One who will determine our eternal fate? Yes. Have they complied with the biblical mandate to ask for His forgiveness for their sins and to acknowledge that He, and He alone, is able to dismiss our failings and gain us entry into God's presence for eternity? Well, in their minds, yes, as evidenced by their church attendance, by their donations to ministry activity and by their acknowledgment of His deity and supremacy.

But, as James 2:19 tells us, even the demons under the command of Satan believe in God and are blown away by the mere thought of His strength and majesty, and yet they remain demons, well-informed but evil and condemned forever. Our dear friends who attend church but who do not understand salvation are little better off than the demons in eternal terms. If their choices continue along their current path, as the odds suggest, their chances of coming to grips with the truth about Christ and their own mortality are slim.

## HEARING AND BELIEVING

To suggest that we have done all that we can and have successfully reached every adult with the gospel message blurs the distinction between *exposure* to the gospel and truly *hearing* the gospel. Just as Jesus had to teach the same

basic lesson to His closest associates again and again, we may have to proclaim the gospel to the same people, time after time, in various contexts,
with a variety applications, before they truly absorb the implications and
importance of what we are sharing.

On the job, I am a living example of the challenge of getting those who
are in the presence of knowledge to translate that knowledge into a meaningful reality. At Barna Research, I am usually swamped, overwhelmed with
project deadlines and pressing client needs that must be satisfied for our
company to perform its obligations.

During the course of a day, it is not unusual for a colleague to warn me
of an approaching deadline for a report or presentation. After a polite nod
of appreciation, I instantly forget the conversation and continue to focus
upon my immediate crises and opportunities.

Eventually, I discover that the aforementioned items are nearly due.
Frantic productivity ensues, but not before I implore my colleagues to be
more deliberate about tracking our delivery dates and to keep me aware of
such important matters.

The team then gently reminds me that the deadline had, in fact, been
brought to my attention and that I had acknowledged receipt of the information through verbal assent.

Was I exposed to the warning? Yes. Did I hear it? No. My employees have
learned that they cannot take for granted that telling me important information means that I have absorbed it, anymore than I may automatically
assume that if I am unaware of a pressing deadline that my colleagues have
failed to inform me of its impending arrival.

## EXPOSURE IS NOT ENOUGH

Influencing people's lives with the message that Christ came to save them
but that they must accept the gift of grace operates in the same manner.
Those who attend church regularly are an unfortunate but prime example of
this principle. They are exposed to the words of the gospel, to exhortations
to accept Christ personally and to invitations to follow the simple steps to
receive Him into their lives. But have they truly heard what is being said?

## WHY THE PITCH OFTEN FAILS

Non-Christians have indicated to us, through survey results, that the communication of the gospel may fail to influence them for three major reasons. One reason is that they do not see the *relevance* of the gospel. A second reason is that they *do not comprehend* what we are trying to say. The
third reason is that the solution provided by the death and resurrection of
Jesus Christ is *so different* from the kinds of solutions they are searching for
as they cruise through life.

Relevance is a big issue in people's lives today. Unless we perceive something to be relevant, we tune it out immediately. To be effective in evangelism, then, one of the hurdles we must clear is the fact that to millions of people, eternal salvation does not seem relevant. In absolute terms, little could be of greater significance. In relative terms, though, being spared from eternal condemnation does not press a "hot button" or address a "felt need."

In a consumption-oriented economy, we are focused upon those stresses and opportunities that require immediate attention and promise immediate results. Discussions about what is likely to happen after we die seem so morbid, so distant, so unrealistic.

In truth, of course, every person on the planet today has a vested interest in where he or she will spend eternity and in the state of comfort that time will be spent. But most people have "pressing matters" on their minds: the fastest route home, how to pay the mortgage, the proper way to discipline their children, the illness that has hospitalized a relative, what the Celtics have to do to make the play-offs. Life after death? Few people consider this an issue of such pressing significance that it merits serious consideration at the moment.

The second reason for rejecting evangelistic pitches surprised me. I discovered that in many cases, nonbelievers have earnestly sought out the answers to meaning in life and the probable outcomes after death. Their inquiries and explorations often have resulted in dead ends, however, because well-intentioned Christians have used impenetrable language and concepts to tell nonbelievers about the world's greatest gift.

When was the last time you tried to listen objectively to how we talk about salvation to a nonbeliever? Try this experiment: Eavesdrop on a Christian sharing his or her faith with a nonbeliever and try to hear it through the filter of the nonbeliever. What you are likely to find is that we communicate the world's greatest story in language that makes no sense to the typical nonbeliever. Think about the words we rely on to communicate the message. Here are a few expressions I drew from some tracts, books and songs that are popular evangelistic tools among Christians. We ask the uninitiated to:

- Be covered by the blood of the Lamb;
- Be fed by the Word;
- Possess a broken spirit;
- Pursue a Christian walk;
- Seek the fellowship of the Holy Spirit;
- Be slain in the Spirit;
- Repent of thy transgressions;
- Do not trust in yourself;
- Prepare for the dawn of the millennial age.

### SPEAKING A SECRET LANGUAGE

These terms mean nothing to someone who is not already deeply indoctrinated in the faith. What we communicate to people by using these words and phrases is that if they don't speak the secret language, they can't be part of the special club. When we use Churchspeak or Christianese, we alienate rather than enlighten people.

It's like traveling to a foreign nation, hearing people speak a foreign language all day and returning to your room at night with a pounding headache and with absolutely no idea what any person said to you at any time during the day. You listened intently but you did not understand a word they said.

The tragedy of this reality hit me several years ago during a Christmas

■ ■

## AMERICANS ARE SEEKING FIRST AND FORE-MOST A DEITY WHO WILL HANDLE THEIR CONSUMER-DRIVEN WANTS, NEEDS, DREAMS, HURTS AND DISAPPOINTMENTS.

■ ■ ■

visit with nonbelieving family members. I sat to watch TV with one of the young men in my extended family. As the screen came to life, it happened to be set on a channel that featured a well-known televangelist speaking to a large crowd.

The televangelist was on a roll, passionately arguing for people to abandon their worldly desires in favor of a life of devotion to Christ and simplicity. I kept the TV on that channel for several minutes, hoping the stirring monologue would provoke some interest or serious conversation with my non-Christian kinfolk. In less than five minutes time, though, he was squirming anxiously in his seat. It was obvious this was not the Holy Spirit bringing my relative under conviction.

In deference to my relative, I grabbed the remote and channel surfed, looking for a program that might satisfy his viewing pleasures. As we flipped through the numerous options, I casually asked what he thought of the portion of the evangelistic message we had heard. His reply summed it up quite succinctly: "What the hell was he talking about?"

From a believer's perspective, I would have applauded the evangelist's eloquent presentation, the fury of emotion, the apparent sincerity with which he made his case. The preacher had said the words that satisfied the convinced (i.e., me) but had failed to effectively communicate with the true target, the confused (i.e., my relative).

### THE MESSAGE IS RADICAL TO NONBELIEVERS

The third reason for rejecting evangelistic pitches is that the message, as a life solution, is radically different from what the nonbeliever expected. Preachers make a great deal of the fact that the Jews at the time of Jesus did not understand His message because they were expecting a political savior, the proverbial warrior on a white stallion, rather than a spiritual savior. Americans today struggle from a similar dilemma: We expect a dominant consumer advocate rather than a spiritual champion.

Every year, my company interviews thousands of Americans about their personal needs and expectations and their spiritual development. Among the many trends we have seen emerge is that when it comes to spirituality, Americans are seeking first and foremost a deity who will handle their consumer-driven wants, needs, dreams, hurts and disappointments. Their concern is in the here and now, not in the hereafter. The pure evangelistic appeal shouts loud and clear to the average adult that the true savior is not to be found in what the Christian faith has to offer.

Jesus saw what was happening during His three years of public ministry and made the adjustment. Instead of debating the Sadducees and Pharisees about doctrinal details, He spent time within the community, discerning people's most pressing concerns, addressing them at their point of felt need, then dispensing the true, lasting solution to the larger issues with which they were also struggling.

He knew He had to attract their attention, to establish His credibility and to provide them with something of value before He could hope to challenge their thinking about the meaning of life on earth or the means to everlasting life and a relationship with the holy and righteous God of Israel. Jesus Himself contextualized His message in such a way that the recipient of His blessings was in tune with the messenger, and ultimately, the message itself.

# IS THE JOB DONE?

So have we saturated America with the gospel?

We may confidently say that most, if not all, adults have been exposed to the gospel of Jesus Christ. We may also suggest that every American has access to the gospel. But we may not conclude that every American has actually heard and understood the gospel. Until we present the message in ways that penetrate the consciousness of the people we seek to influence for Christ, we have not truly communicated. We have only made noise.

Granted, we are not responsible for the choices other people make, and some will hear the gospel and will consciously reject it. We do, however, have a responsibility to present the gospel in a fashion that can be understood, clearly and easily.

Further, our discussion has focused predominantly on efforts to reach adults, a target audience where the American Church has concentrated its evangelism resources. But what about the 70 million individuals under the age of 18? Should we be concerned about reaching them with the good news of Christ's work on earth?

The humanitarian answer is "by all means, children are human beings who deserve the same care as older people." The research response would be "certainly because studies show that most people accept Jesus Christ as their Savior before they reach the age of 18."[5]

The strategic perspective would exhort us to reach out to children today because a new, potentially larger wave of youngsters will soon be on the way, and besides, today's children are tomorrow's leaders and decision-makers. And Jesus' reply would be a compassionate, "Let the little children come to me, and do not hinder them, for the kingdom of heaven belongs to such as these" (Matt. 19:14).

Yet another consideration is the increasing flow of non-English speaking people into the United States. Nearly one million foreign-born people immigrate to this country every year. Hundreds of thousands of those immigrants speak English as a second language, if at all. Do they have easy access to the gospel in a language and style that resonates with them? Currently, 32 million people in America speak some language other than English as their primary language.[6] This represents a new and rapidly growing mission field on our home soil.

For my money, the answer to the question "Have we saturated America with the gospel?" is a resounding no. We still have much ground to cover. We have the means to do so. Do we have the will?

NOTES
1. "Evangelicals" is a much-used, little-understood term. To the secular media, it typically means right-wing religious fanatics. In my writings, the term refers to people who meet several criteria. These are people who have an orthodox Judeo-Christian definition of God; rely solely upon the grace of God through the Person of Jesus Christ for their salvation; believe that Satan is a real being, not merely symbolic; contend that a person is incapable of earning eternal salvation; believe that the Bible is accurate in all of its teachings; and believe that they personally have a responsibility to share their religious faith with others who believe differently. Currently, evangelicals represent a bit less than 10 percent of the national population, according to this battery of criteria.

2. These figures are from a nationwide survey of adults by the Barna Research Group, Ltd. conducted in January 1994. We interviewed a random sample of 1,206 adults and included open-ended questions in which we asked them, without any prompting or list to choose from, to describe what these words meant to them.

3. A born-again Christian in this book refers to anyone who claims to have made "a personal commitment to Jesus Christ that is still important in their lives today" and who, when given seven choices about life after death, selects the option that says: "When I die, I will go to heaven because I have confessed my sins and have accepted Jesus Christ as my Savior." In reality, there is no distinction between a "born-again" Christian and a Christian—you either are or are not a Christian. I use the term "born again," however, to distinguish between those who have made a decision to follow Christ as opposed to "cultural Christians"—the majority of Americans who may go to church, read the Bible and say they believe in Christ but have yet to make Him their sole means of salvation.

4. This is a consistent finding that has emerged in our studies in the past six years. Each year, we conduct two large nationwide surveys of adults. Typically, we discover that about half of all of those who had attended church during the week prior to the survey were not Christian. The figure was typically in the 51 percent to 54 percent range in the early 1990s. Recently, because of the exodus of the baby boomers from Protestant churches, the number has dipped into the 47 percent to 51 percent range.

5. This statistic is from several national studies we have conducted. We find that about two-thirds of all adults who are born again made their decision to follow Christ before they reached the age of 18.

6. The U.S. Census Bureau reports that 32 million people age five or older speak a language other than English as their primary tongue in their homes. This equates to 14 percent of the national population.

# 3

# REACHING PEOPLE WHO ARE OUTSIDE THE TENT

For the past decade, we have been tracking the size of the adult population that does not attend church or religious services.[1] Since the beginning of the 1990s, the proportion of the adult population that is nonchurched has risen significantly, to 32 percent from about 25 percent.[2] That may not sound like much, but 32 percent of the 195 million adults in America equals 60 million to 65 million people. Add the children of those people and the total is more than 80 million people.

To put this statistic into context, the nonchurched population of America would be equivalent to the 11th largest nation in the world—larger than any nation in Europe, three times the population of Canada, more than double the population of California.[3]

Missions organizations spend billions of dollars recruiting, training and sending Americans to nations where the missionary does not speak the native language, understand the local customs or have strong relationships or support systems. Although such global vision and outreach is laudable, it is imperative to recognize that tens of millions of our friends and neighbors constitute one of the more extensive mission fields in the world.

## THE BOOMER EXIT

As we survey our local communities, we learn that an increasing number of people are avoiding—and leaving—religious centers. We discover, for example, the recent exodus of many baby boomers.[4] During the 1960s and 1970s, a generation called the boomers rebelled against most things that smacked of tradition, stability or the status quo. Organized religion was one of their targets.

In the mid-1980s, however, after nearly two decades of revolt against traditional religious beliefs and practices, we witnessed a dramatic turnaround in which millions of boomers returned to churches.

In some cases, the return was precipitated by the challenges of marriage, something that many boomers put off until they were established in a life pattern and then found sharing their lives with a partner more difficult. The hope was that perhaps they could find common ground, relational principles or a relational context through involvement in religion.

For an even larger proportion of boomers, the birth of their children stimulated their pilgrimage back to the Church. Although they personally had not found religion to be particularly helpful in their developmental years, they now struggled as parents to expose their children to a holistic values system and plausible worldview.

Anxious to do what was best for their children, millions of parents hoped that the religious training provided by churches would help fill the values void experienced by their youngsters. For still millions of other boomers, the motivation to return to church was based upon their desperate and continuing searches for significant life values and for a sense of meaning and purpose in life.

Having spent the better part of two decades exploring materialism, utilitarianism, consumerism and agnosticism, these people felt there must be something bigger, something better, something more pure or something more substantive than the vacuous reality they had been experiencing for so long.

## THE RETREAT STARTED IN 1991

After several years of honest efforts to see what the Christian Church had to offer, though, boomers began a massive retreat from churches starting in 1991. Our exit interviews indicate that most of them departed because their churches promised more than they delivered. These spiritual seekers did not truly find the relationships, the wisdom and worldview, or the personal benefits they had expected.

I believe the timing of the boomers' exodus was no coincidence. Think of all the cataclysmic events that took place within a year or so of the boomer exodus. The demise of the Soviet empire. The spread of AIDS, made real to heterosexuals for the first time by Magic Johnson's announcement of having the virus. The economic woes of the United States, resulting in a minor depression. The Gulf War. The nasty and ideologically confusing presidential election campaign between Bill Clinton, George Bush and Ross Perot. Irangate.

So many challenging activities happening virtually simultaneously caused millions of people to question what was important and reliable in their lives and to rid themselves of the baggage of relationships, lifestyles and other commitments that were not productive. During the tough evaluation period, Christian churches were deemed by more than 4 million boomers to be irrelevant and disappointing. The action step that followed was to cut their tenuous ties with those churches.

But the story of the nonchurched people of America transcends the spiritual flirting of the boomers. Boomers represent about 42 percent of the adults who are not aligned with a church—a substantial proportion, but not even a majority of the religiously disaffected. The entire group of people who avoid churches differs in many ways from the church-going population. Those who reject church activity have different demographic attributes, different worldviews and unique perspectives on religion and church life.

## DISPARATE DEMOGRAPHICS
For openers, nonchurched adults have a disparate demographic profile. As you might expect, men are much more likely than women to have no active church connections. Our latest surveys show that 61 percent of all nonchurched people are men while 39 percent are women.

With the departure of so many boomers, we have seen the average age of nonchurched adults rise significantly. Although the nonchurched had tended to be younger than average, they are now a reflection of the adult population. The median age of adults who avoid organized religious activity is 39, which is actually a few years older than the national median for adults (37).

Oddly, although the nonchurched are more likely than most people to have completed a college education (31 percent), they do not have higher household income levels. This is partially because a majority of the nonchurched are single. Presently, 53 percent are single (compared to 45 percent in the United States), divided almost evenly between those who have never been married and those who have been divorced. Caucasians are more likely than nonwhites to reject church life.

In short, the nonchurched population tends to be fairly mature, sophisticated, well-trained for cultural ascendancy and independence, and not involved in a traditional family experience. Our studies show that the nonchurched have personality and temperament traits that typically accompany being upscale and unattached—they tend to be aggressive, energetic, skeptical, experimental and transitory.

Put differently, they are not the kinds of people that churches would ordinarily identify as a prime-target population. But they are the mission field.

## BEEN THERE, DONE THAT
One of the most riveting revelations is that most nonchurched people were

churched at some point in their lives. They are not merely unchurched; most have literally been *de-churched*. Overall, 85 percent of all nonchurched adults have had a prolonged period of time during which they consistently attended a church or religious center. Few adults living in America today have never had a serious and protracted church experience.

What makes this realization so powerful is that adults attend church of their own volition. For people to leave, they often must be driven away. The de-churched admitted that if the church they had been attending had understood them and ministered to them effectively, they would have stayed. Further, this information tells us that if we hope to attract the de-churched back into the fold, it will take more than opening the doors and welcoming them in.

We are not simply starting at square one, as if these were an irreligious people who had never experienced what the church has to offer, seen how it operates or been disappointed by its performance. They have seen it, heard it, felt it. Before we can hope to attract the de-churched, we must address the past shortcomings they have experienced and move them beyond those concerns toward a more fulfilling and useful relationship with God and His people.

Driving people away is not just a characteristic of conservative churches or liberal churches, evangelical congregations or mainline congregations. It is a reality that affects all churches. Our investigation showed that those churches that fared best at retaining people were nondenominational churches, evangelical denominational churches other than Southern Baptist, Assemblies of God and Mormon churches.[5]

We also found that churches that have 200 or more adults attending their weekend services were less likely to lose adherents than were those with smaller average turnouts. This is consistent with the current trend toward midsize and larger churches, the attraction being the heightened ability to meet the spectrum of needs within the congregation—whether that ability is real or simply perceived.

## REASONS FOR REJECTION

When you scrape away all the excuses and niceties, most nonchurched people avoid church involvement because they fail to see any compelling reason to invest the time and energy in the exercise. Having been involved in church life for a prolonged period of time, their cost-benefit analysis has determined that they do not get enough positive benefits from church participation to merit their continued involvement.

We also learned that most nonchurched adults have several reasons why they stopped attending church. The rare person identifies just one reason for pulling back. When we ask these people to identify the central justification for their decision to quit the church, however, the main response invariably relates to the belief that churches have nothing of real benefit to offer.

Whether we like it or not, adults have been trained to survive our culture by evaluating their experiences and relationships in terms of the positive personal benefits received. Those engagements that do not supply them with a sufficient degree of perceived value are dismissed unceremoniously.

It's a competitive world out there. Perhaps four or five decades ago people would grit their teeth and bear an unsatisfying or unfulfilling church experience. Today, however, we are liberated from traditions, loyalties, commitments and societal expectations. It's every person for himself or herself. Whichever life options are readily available to the person and promise the most appealing and pleasing set of outcomes will win the momentary allegiance of the typical adult, regardless of the long-term consequences or effects of their choices.

■ ■

IN OUR CULTURE, THE THRUST IS TO ENHANCE SELF-ESTEEM, SELF-PRESERVATION, SELF-PROTECTION, SELF-FULFILLMENT, SELF-PROMOTION AND SELF-DEVELOPMENT. INVOLVEMENT WITH A CHURCH IS BASED ON WHAT THE CHURCH CAN DO FOR THE PERSON, NOT WHAT THE PERSON CAN DO FOR THE CHURCH.

■ ■ ■

Nonchurched people describe their disinterest in churches in many ways. The most common reasons given are that they are too busy (an explanation that is merely a smoke screen for being disinterested, a reason given by 42 percent). They believe the church has nothing of value to offer (40 percent). They visited churches but never found one of interest (38 percent). They prefer to pursue other activities on their families' days off (35 percent). They are unaware of any churches they would like to try (33 percent). They have yet to find any churches whose theology and doctrine parallels their own (33 percent). They believe that their lifestyles would be incompatible with the expectations of the church (31 percent).

Analyze these reasons carefully and you will find that a single thread runs through most of them. Simply stated, people expect a church to conform to the will, needs or interests of the individual person. Nonchurched people would define a healthy, compelling church as one that does whatever is necessary to satisfy the tangible needs of the person; that is, they take self-centered approaches to defining the role of the church. Few nonchurched adults think of the church as the pivotal player in this drama with the attender following a prescribed role for a predetermined purpose.

It is easy to understand this perspective. In our culture, the thrust is to enhance self-esteem, self-preservation, self-protection, self-fulfillment, self-promotion and self-development. In this context, involvement with a church is based on what the church can do for the person, not what the person can do for the church.

Being an active participant in a community of faith is more likely to infer the expectation of emotional gratification or physical assistance than a selfless focus on spiritual development. Perhaps most amazing of all is the reality that those people who regularly attend churches and participate in the lives of the congregations have found ways of integrating the focus on personal needs with the investment in the health of the churches. Perhaps achieving that balance is a sign of spiritual maturity, a level of maturity that the nonchurched have yet to reach.

## A RAY OF HOPE

In spite of their personal decisions to exempt themselves from organized religious activities, nonchurched adults have not wiped religion out of their lives altogether. For instance, we found that almost one-third of the nonchurched (30 percent) say that religion is very important in their lives, and another one-third (34 percent) describe it as somewhat important.

When it comes to the definition of their faith views, we discovered that most nonchurched people think of themselves as Christian, or as having an affinity for the Christian faith. One-third (34 percent) said they have very favorable impressions of Christianity, and an additional one-third said they possess somewhat favorable views of Christianity.

The problem becomes more serious when respondents talked about the local church. Only one out of every four nonchurched adults (25 percent) claimed to have a very favorable impression of the Christian churches in their area, and an additional one-third said they have somewhat favorable impressions of those churches.

The conclusion we may draw from these attitudes is that the nonchurched are generally open to religious thought, activity and expression. In fact, most of them have positive views of the Christian faith. The stumbling block comes down to experiencing that faith in a church setting. Based on their past experiences as well as their current needs and expectations and in spite of their esteem for Christianity, the typical nonchurched adult is not predisposed to assume that a local church is capable of delivering on the promises of Christianity and of making the faith come alive.

For a church to attract such a person, then, requires bucking the odds. It can be done—indeed, it is done every day—but it is the exception to the rule. It takes creativity, perseverance, pure motives, intelligent strategy and careful interaction to pull it off.

## THE OUTSIDER'S PERSPECTIVE

Many church leaders with whom I work struggle to understand the divergent worldviews and perspectives of nonbelievers. As you think about the nonchurched people you know, keep in mind that when we speak about fundamental spiritual principles and Christian factors, they are using an entirely different filter for perceiving the world.

For instance, most Christians would say that if they moved to a new location, they would search for a church and base a significant degree of their choice upon the religious beliefs of the churches they visit. That's not the case with the nonchurched. Only one-third of the nonchurched regard the religious beliefs of the church as one of the single, most important considerations.

Overall, only half of the nonchurched define doctrinal stands as one of the two or three most important considerations. In fact, one out of every five nonchurched adults state that the theological beliefs of the church simply would not be important in selecting a church.

The spiritual perspective of the typical nonchurched person further underscores just how different that person views the role, the value and the choice of a church. Only half of them describe God as the all-powerful, all-knowing Creator of the world who still rules it today. The other half have a variety of unbiblical perceptions of who or what God is or how many deities exist. And while almost half of those who attend church services are born-again Christians, just 17 percent of the nonchurched are trusting Christ alone for their salvation.

This raises an interesting point. If more than 60 million adults are nonchurched, and 17 percent of them are born-again believers, then more than 10 million born-again adults do not have a church home! Imagine what it would mean to bring the wayward believers back to the community of saints. If these people were evenly divided among the existing Protestant churches in America, each church would reap a harvest of 33 new attenders. That would increase the size of the average congregation by almost 33 percent—more growth than most churches have seen in years.

As additional evidence that these nonchurched adults are not opposed to religion, we learned that most of them have some form of personal involvement in religious communications or development. One out of every 4 nonchurched people reads the Bible during a typical month. The same proportion is engaged in reading a religious book or magazine and in watching a religious television program during a typical month. One out of 5 nonchurched adults listens to a religious radio program during the month. And 7 out of 10 pray to God each month.

This is not the profile of the rabidly religious. Neither, however, is it the profile of a population that is wholeheartedly disinterested in spiritual matters. They are keeping their foot in the door. It just isn't the door of a church.

## PRESSING THE HOT BUTTONS

Like it or not, the nonchurched population is perhaps most open to religion if it can help solve some of their problems or address some of their most pressing needs. But what are those needs and interests?

Undoubtedly, the list changes as a person's life develops. In terms of general categories, however, we learned that by far the most pressing issue confronting nonchurched people is their financial condition. One out of every three nonchurched adults stated that he or she was struggling with a financial problem—not enough money to pay the bills, not making enough money at a job, cannot pay off debts, cannot afford the basics of life and so forth. Even the next most common concern—employment status—was an economic issue. These initial two issues concern half of all nonchurched people. The message: If you want to get their attention, help them deal with their financial struggles.

Only two other aspects of life were mentioned as particularly problematic by at least 1 out of every 10 nonchurched adults. Personal health was one. Ten percent said they are afflicted with health problems that limited their lifestyle and left them emotionally frustrated.

The other issue was related to family matters, which was mentioned by 11 percent of the nonchurched segment. Half of these related to issues of child rearing—discipline, communication, single-parenting difficulties and school-related concerns.

The other half were spread over a broad spectrum of items, such as improving the husband-wife relationship, making family a priority and learning how to enjoy family time, and addressing the needs of their aging parents.

Interestingly, when you ask nonchurched people to identify their most vexing issue, *less than 1 percent of them identify any issue of spiritual nature to be their core concern.* Very small numbers of people think of the quality of their relationship with God, their involvement in a community of faith, their understanding of their religious heritage, or the development of their personal belief system or anything related to their spirituality to be the central difficulty with which they are preoccupied.

Do you see the clashing worlds of the typical church leader and the typical nonchurched person? Ask those people who set the evangelistic agenda of the church to identify the lead issues and concerns to be addressed and what do you hear? Relationship with God, spiritual beliefs, morality, values, salvation by grace, biblical knowledge, purity of worship, commitment to service, praising God and seeking forgiveness through Christ. Every one of these aspects of personal and corporate spiritual growth is of tantamount importance. And not one of these factors is on the minds of the nonchurched. Should they be? Undoubtedly. Can these factors win a place at the top of the mental and emotional agenda of the nonchurched by virtue of a church saying that these should be the priority issues?

Look at the playing field through the lenses of the nonchurched. The very issues these people raise as their most pressing concerns—financial anxieties and needs—often are dismissed by churches and church leaders as a diversion from the real heart of human need and struggle. Churches tend to downplay the importance of money and financial focus for fear of promoting materialism, consumerism, greed, competition, errant views of success and the like. The message is interpreted by millions of nonchurched people as "they don't understand or they don't care about my struggles. They're into their own agenda—beliefs, values, morals—that is far from where I'm at. The church has nothing to offer me today."

If you analyze the issues and programs that churches address most often—spiritual purity and commitment, family focus and enhancement—it becomes clear that most church services and programs are not designed to speak to the needs and interests of those who are outside the church looking in. We proudly and consistently emphasize the significance of spiritual maturity and family priorities as keys to a joyful and meaningful life, as perhaps we should.

One consequence of that focus is to ignore the perspectives and dominant felt needs of the growing contingent of nonchurched people. If reaching these people is truly a goal of the church—and that is a major and very important "if"—then we must rethink the strategies we are relying upon for influencing their thinking and behavior.

To church people, speaking about matters such as godliness, purity, righteousness, the integration of the spiritual disciplines in our daily lives, practicing forgiveness and love, and preaching salvation by grace are good, proper and necessary.

To a huge proportion of the population—the people who live outside the boundaries of the church—these are secondary matters. They appear to be issues that would only concern the rich, the frivolous or the ignorant. The "real" issues of life in their view relate to finding a decent job, putting food on the table, maintaining a good credit record, earning a measure of job security and making enough money to live comfortably. From this vantage point, to address anything else is irrelevant.

### A CASE IN POINT
The statement of one person who stopped attending churches recently sums up this perspective:

"I got tired of hearing sermons about being nice to other people, or how important it is to read the Bible or give money to the church so they could bring in more people who could be told to be nice to other people and read the Bible.

■ ■

## BEFRIENDING GOD...IS IMPORTANT TO MOST AMERICANS, EVEN FOR THOSE WHO DO NOT SEE THE VALUE OF CHURCH LIFE.

■ ■ ■

"I've got three kids at home who don't have nice clothing, who don't get a vacation trip every year, who have never been to Disney World. They don't see much of me or their dad because we're working ourselves silly to make ends meet. Sure, it's great to be nice to your neighbors and to be understanding when others mistreat you.

"But that's not the problem in my life. I am tired, lonely, on the edge financially, and I don't see any light at the end of the tunnel. I don't really care about choirs, short-term missions trips, youth-group events or men's breakfast groups. I'm drowning in the whirlpool of life's realities. The church isn't helping me. And like they say, if it ain't part of the solution, then it must be part of the problem."

### LIFE PRIORITIES
To get a clear understanding of the relative importance of various aspects of life, we asked nonchurched adults to rate the significance of 13 life conditions or outcomes. Their responses underscore what is important to them. Their priorities are shown in Table 3.1.

By far the most important consideration is having good health. Nine out of 10 Americans who do not attend a church say good health is very important to them. The next echelon of important factors includes having close, personal friendships (rated very important by 74 percent), having a comfortable lifestyle (71 percent) and having a clear purpose for living (71 percent). Notice that those elements coincide with some of the basic life needs that psychologists tell us human beings innately pursue: physical, emotional and intellectual comfort and wholeness. All that's missing is spiritual wholeness.

The next level of concerns encompasses factors that are of moderate importance to the nonchurched. Those concerns include living to an old age (very important to 53 percent), living close to family and relatives (51 percent), having a close relationship with God (49 percent) and having an active sex life (48 percent).

The encouraging truth that emerges here is that half of all nonchurched adults assert that having a meaningful relationship with God is significant to them. Three out of four nonchurched people (73 percent) describe this as either very or somewhat important. Befriending God, then, is important to most Americans, even for those who do not see the value of church life.

This odd juxtapositioning—appreciating God but intentionally avoiding church—is confirmed by the fact that being part of a local church was viewed as being a very desirable life condition by just 15 percent of the nonchurched and a somewhat desirable outcome among another 28 percent. To most Americans, being well-known is not nearly as critical as being comfortable and secure. Neither fame nor involvement in a church, however, is viewed as accomplishing people's true goals.

## TABLE 3.1

## LIFE CONDITIONS THAT ARE VERY DESIRABLE

### A COMPARISON OF THE VIEWS OF CHURCHED AND NONCHURCHED ADULTS

|  | Percent Who Said This Is Very Desirable | |
| --- | --- | --- |
| Life Condition | Churched | Nonchurched |
| Having good health | 91% | 91% |
| Having close, personal friendships | 79 | 74 |
| Having a clear purpose for living | 82 | 71 |
| Having a comfortable lifestyle | 72 | 71 |
| Living to an old age | 57 | 53 |
| Living close to family and relatives | 65 | 51 |
| Having a close relationship with God | 86 | 49 |
| Having an active sex life | 49 | 48 |
| Having a high-paying job | 42 | 39 |
| Influencing other people's lives | 42 | 28 |
| Owning a large home | 29 | 28 |
| Being part of a local church | 64 | 15 |
| Achieving fame or public recognition | 10 | 9 |

(NOTE: This table is based upon interviews with national samples of 301 nonchurched adults and 509 churched adults.)

## LIGHTING THE FIRE

Although most nonchurched adults were less than enthusiastic about seeking a church home, they agreed that five arguments might convince them to try a church, assuming the argument is properly communicated and sufficiently backed up.

The first of the potentially appealing arguments is that they could truly experience God. Two out of every three nonchurched adults called this a compelling motivation. Yet, as I have talked with church leaders regarding this outcome, they have challenged the validity of the research.

"All they want is to experience God?" they ask. "Why, that's what we do every time we get together as a church. We are constantly revealing more about God's nature and character and about His exhortations to us. We worship God, we praise Him, we pray to Him. We expose God to people through the lives of people whom He has touched. Clearly, these people are pulling your leg, telling you what they think you want to hear. If that's what they really wanted, they could have it, abundantly, right now, as our church is."

Unfortunately, the assumption that "they could have it, abundantly, right now, as our church is" is a barrier to reaching the unreached. What we believe we provide people through our church activities and what the recipients believe they receive are often two different things.

Preaching about God, reading the Bible together, leading public prayers and challenging people to honor God through our thoughts and lifestyles is *not* what the nonchurched (and, it turns out, what millions of churched people) construe to be "knowing God." They want a deeper, more tangible and significant experience with God.

It is the difference between hearing *about* God and interacting *with* Him directly. To emphasize the point, we recently surveyed churched people who describe themselves as Christian, Protestant or Catholic and asked how often they experience the presence of God at their churches. Among these church regulars, nearly two out of every three (61 percent) said they sense God's presence only occasionally, rarely or never. What they typically get is an experience with people who talk about and hope to interact with God. That is a world apart from experiencing God Himself.[6]

A second driving motivation for the nonchurched would be the provision of valuable religious teaching or training for their children. Three out of four parents of children under the age of 18 said a church that could truly deliver such assistance would be of interest to them. Among parents of children under 18, no single motivation ranked higher on their lists than the provision of religious training for their children.

Again, I consistently hear church leaders tell me that their churches are already emphasizing family and are providing programs such as Sunday School, midweek youth activities and other special events for youth. But we have to hear the message shouted at us by parents who are outside of the church: They have found that the existing teaching and programs simply do not provide what they are seeking.

What churches are doing might be educationally sound and spiritually helpful. The bottom line, however, is that the "target customer," so to speak, is not satisfied with the product. The customer has a continuing felt need for the right product, but will not become active in a church that does not provide that product, according to the specifications that the consumer defines.

The last three items that would attract the nonchurched are providing a better and more practical understanding of the Bible; offering a nonthreatening environment in which they could meet other people who live in their community; and discovering better ways of dealing with their everyday problems.

Just more than half of all nonchurched people said that each of these factors would be a convincing reason to attend a church. Notice that each of these items provides tangible, personally valuable assistance toward leading a more satisfying and meaningful life. Millions of nonchurched people admitting they would attend a church if it offered these elements suggests that they have yet to encounter a religious body that makes these services readily available.

You may be interested in the reasons nonchurched people gave that would not prove to be compelling to attend a church: Meeting people like themselves; attending because other people's lives have been changed through their church-based experiences; discovering why other people are serious about and involved in religious pursuits; protesting themselves against the possible wrath or judgment of God; trying out church services that are different from the typical traditional services; and making family or friends happy by attending a church.

## THE DREAM CHURCH

Although many nonchurched would not initiate their involvement with a church by attending a Sunday service, they would eventually wind up incorporating their assessment of the worship service as a critical factor in their decision of sticking with a particular church or choosing another course of action.

The worship service, which Christians generally think of as the most important aspect in the decision of a nonchurched person to return to church, turns out to be just one of several key elements in that decision. For many nonchurched people, it is not the most important factor.

Nevertheless, the worship service remains the centerpiece of most church ministries.

Most nonchurched adults would prefer a service that incorporates traditional hymns rather than contemporary Christian music. This surprises many people, who assume that anything that smacks of tradition is automatically rejected by those who are outside the church. The truth is that nonchurched adults are twice as likely to say they would prefer traditional hymns to contemporary forms of music.

One caution must be raised, however—other research we have conducted shows that most adults have never heard contemporary Christian music. When they are attempting to describe the kind of music they would prefer, what we really are hearing is that half would like the known—hymns— while the other half would like something different, whatever it might sound like or be called. The nonchurched are also divided about whether they want a lot or just a little music in the service.

By a margin of more than 2-to-1, the nonchurched would prefer an informal service. This relates to the use of robes; the style of language (i.e., archaic English as found in the *King James Version* of the Bible versus the more comfortable language in recent translations); the style of dress of the congregation; and the overall environment established in the service.

Half of the nonchurched people said they would prefer a service that did not include a live dramatic presentation; one-third said they would prefer such a drama. Most people also indicated a preference for live announcements of church activities rather than a videotaped presentation. We again found, however, that few of the nonchurched had ever attended a service that included video presentations, so they were basing their decisions upon assumptions of the quality and appeal of videotaped announcements.

Perhaps the most surprising revelation regarding the kind of church nonchurched people would like to attend related to the size of the congregation. By almost a three-to-one margin, they would rather attend a church of fewer than 200 people (61 percent) than a church of 200 or more (22 percent). This was unexpected, given the recent growth in the number and size of megachurches, bodies that attract 2,000 or more people to their weekend services.

Why would the first choice of the nonchurched be a relatively small church? Three dominant reasons emerge: It would be easier to meet other people; they would receive a greater degree of personal attention; and it would be easier to get involved and make a difference in the church.

Why, then, do most nonchurched people who return to the church wind up attaching themselves to larger churches? Again, the three primary reasons are: People in larger churches are more likely to invite the nonchurched to visit; the programs and opportunities at larger churches are more extensive and of higher quality; and larger churches tend to exhibit more energy and openness to outsiders. In other words, larger churches address three critical desires of the modern American adult: The opportunity to make choices from a menu of alternatives; to participate in a high-quality experience; and to be part of a comfortable atmosphere.

Are small churches able to meet these needs? Obviously, the answer is yes, otherwise we would not see the growth of many small churches that eventually blossom into megachurches. At the same time, however, it must be noted that most churches never grow to a size of 200 people. The average church in the United States consists of 102 adults. Thus, it is possible for a small church to be appealing to visitors, but the law of averages is against that likelihood.

## NOTES

1. Throughout this book, I refer to nonchurched and de-churched people as those who have not attended a religious service at a church, synagogue or other religious center during the past six months, except for special events such as a wedding or a funeral.
2. The statistics used in this chapter related to nonchurched people are drawn from a nationwide study of nonchurched adults we conducted in August 1993. The study involved extensive interviews with 607 nonchurched adults. This was the third in a series of large nationwide surveys among random samples of nonchurched people conducted over the course of 10 years, enabling us to identify changes in behavioral and attitudinal patterns related to church activity.
3. The only countries that have larger populations are Bangladesh, Brazil, China, India, Indonesia, Japan, Mexico, Nigeria, Pakistan and Russia.
4. Baby boomers are the nation's largest generation ever. These are the 76 million people born between 1946 and 1964. The generation that follows the boomers is commonly known as the baby busters. Busters represent the second largest generation in our history as determined by the births from 1965 to 1983. For more information about the characteristics of the busters, consult George Barna, *Baby Busters: The Disillusioned Generation* (Chicago: Northfield Publishing, 1994).
5. This citation of the Mormon church is not meant to imply that it is a Christian church. It is not. However, when we asked people about the churches they used to attend, we evaluated all churches and faith groups. The Mormon church is mentioned simply because it emerged as one of the few denominations that seemed to beat the averages in terms of attender retention.
6. More about this phenomenon is described in a previous book that discussed some of these research findings. See George Barna, *Virtual America* (Ventura, Calif.: Regal Books, 1994); pp. 55-58, 326-329.

# 4

# EFFECTIVELY MARKETING THE MINISTRY

It is entirely possible that your church has what it takes to be a great church home for many nonchurched people. But it takes more than having the right heart and conditions. The nonchurched must know you exist and must be motivated to check out your church.

The most effective way of getting people to evaluate your church is for you to invite the nonchurched people you know and with whom you have a good relationship. We know this because a majority of the nonchurched people we interviewed told us so. Our studies among church visitors confirms that most people drop in because a trusted friend invited them. And surveys and market testing of other approaches have shown that nothing compares with the effectiveness of the personal touch.

## WHAT TURNS OFF THE NONCHURCHED

Our studies also have identified several activities that are more likely to turn off the nonchurched rather than to get them interested or excited about your church. Calling people on the telephone to invite them, commonly known as telemarketing, leaves a bad taste in the mouths of most nonchurched people. A relative handful of people might follow through and attend, but the negative fallout is so substantial that telemarketing often represents bad stewardship and shortsighted evangelism.

The other tactic that has as great a potential to sour nonchurched adults on a church experience is visiting their homes uninvited. This act creates a measurable hostility toward the Christian faith and its churches.[1]

Why should aggressive marketing, such as telemarketing or home visitation, generate such negative reactions by the nonchurched? For the same reasons that telemarketing or door-to-door salespeople create negative responses. When we engage in such efforts, we are sending the message that our agenda is more important than their privacy and their time. We are imposing our values upon them.

In absolute terms, having a life-changing relationship with God, through the act of sacrifice performed on the cross by Jesus Christ, is more important than whatever they might be doing in their fortress at the time of the contact. But to the nonchurched person, who sees life through a different filter, the contact is simply another example of religious fanatics seeking to force their views on other people.

## What Turns On the Nonchurched

Of the many approaches we have tested through surveys and through evaluating the actual experience of churches, we have learned that only two strategies seem to consistently appeal to the nonchurched.

The first, and most successful, is for churched people to build honest, caring relationships with nonchurched people and eventually to invite them to attend the church. The second is for the church to sponsor nonreligious events such as sports leagues, community fairs, social extravaganzas, community assistance projects, and concerts or seminars of interest to the nonchurched, and to invite those who attend the activities to consider attending the church's services.

A third possibility is sending top-quality brochures about the church to people's homes to inform them and to invite them to attend the church. The results vary substantially, depending upon the quality of the brochure, the timing of mailing, the nature of the appeal, the region of the country, the kind of church sponsoring the mailing and the kind of people who are the targeted recipients of the mailing.

Much has also been said about, and spent on, media advertising to attract the nonchurched. In short, during the past decade, studies we have conducted nationally and in a range of individual geographic markets have consistently shown that advertising may effectively *inform* people of the existence of the church and may also *position* the church in a positive light. Advertising, however, does not *motivate* people to change their existing behavioral pattern to include church attendance or to embrace Christ as their Savior. Advertising can set up a personal contact and thus make it more efficient, but the advertising message rarely has the same power as a one-on-one interaction based on the proven care and credibility associated with the communicator of the church's message.

# JUST THE FACTS

The nonchurched are interested in what happens in churches, especially if they have reason to believe that a church might enhance their quality of life. The message has its greatest thrust when delivered by someone they know and trust, when the statements about the church are believable and when the promises are reasonable.

We found that the nonchurched are interested in discovering four things about a church they are considering attending. The following are the things they want to know:

## 1. DOCTRINE AND BELIEFS

To the typical nonchurched person, this does not mean an intensive exposition of the theological positions of the church. Matters such as predestination, millennialism, soteriology, eschatology and other unpronounceable teachings of the church are the last things they want to hear about.

Focusing on such matters is more likely to repulse rather than to attract the nonchurched. Simply, they want to know if it is a Christian church, a cult or a non-Christian religion. Remember what they are striving to do—to lead a more pleasing, fulfilling and successful life. In essence, they are seeking an understanding of the religious core of the church—little more, nothing less.

## 2. DENOMINATIONAL AFFILIATION

This can cut both ways. Some seekers want to know about denominational affiliation because they were reared in particular kinds of churches and are most likely to return to those churches. Others, however, were reared within particular denominations and are open to attending churches of any denominations other than the ones with which they were previously associated.

Most nonchurched adults have opinions about each of the major denominations and our research shows that those opinions are generally unfavorable. Discovering the denominational affiliation of a given church may work for or against the church. As the nonchurched adult does his or her homework about a church before deciding whether to attend it, the denominational association of the congregation is treated as a clue to what the nonchurched might expect to experience at the church.

## 3-4. LOCATION AND SCHEDULE

If the nonchurched were to return to church, they do not want to stick out like sore thumbs upon their visits. They want to blend in and experience the church as it truly is. Consequently, they are interested in the exact locations and times of the services so they neither become frustrated by getting lost on the journeys to the churches, nor make spectacles of themselves by entering after the proceedings have begun.

We also were told about things they really don't care about. For example, they aren't interested in what the church used to be like. Their response might be: "I want to know what I'm going to experience if I go there, not what my grandparents might have experienced." And they aren't impressed by how many people attend the church. A typical response: "Look, I'm

■ ■

## NONCHURCHED PEOPLE, LIKE MOST AMERI-CANS, WISH TO RETAIN CONTROL OF THEIR EXPERIENCES AND CIRCUMSTANCES.

■ ■ ■

probably only going to go if one of my best friends convinces me to go with them. As long as they're with me, kind of as a security blanket, then it doesn't really matter how many other people are there, does it?"

We also learned that fewer than one out of every five nonchurched adults has any interest in discovering the sermon topic or title, the name or background of the pastor, the availability of child care (it is assumed to exist and to be top-notch) or why other people attend the church.

## ABUSIVE BEHAVIOR

Adults possess many fears about returning to church. One of those is what they may be expected to do to fit in with the crowd. The nonchurched are not interested in being changed. They want positive experiences, but on their terms. Churches that have demonstrated the greatest ability to attract—and to retain—the nonchurched are those that understand the dynamics of visitors' expectations and boundaries.

The two most important experiences visitors can have at your church, by their own reckoning, is to be treated the same as everyone else and to be genuinely welcomed after the service. Four out of five nonchurched adults pine for such an experience.

Visitors, however, generally wish to remain anonymous. When they are ready to be known by the church, they will take the appropriate steps. Nonchurched people, like most Americans, wish to retain control of their experiences and circumstances. Enabling them to visit under the comfort and security of anonymity and then to experience a genuine rather than a staged or forced outpouring of acceptance from the people is likely to impress them favorably.

Our research has determined that non-Christians who are seeking a church home are less interested in the content of the sermon than they are in the heart of the congregation. The first several times they visit a church—if, indeed, they have a sufficiently favorable experience to prompt more than one visit—they are most interested in *feeling* the pulse of the congregation than in *understanding* the doctrine of the body.

The nonchurched have to feel welcome, to feel that this is a group of people with whom they will connect, to feel as if they would be proud to be associated with this Body of people. Once the emotional hurdle is cleared, the person will listen more intently to content and will decide whether spiritual growth is possible.

A number of actions may undermine the efforts of the church to meet the expectations of the unchurched. Negative reactions may arise from trying to make visitors feel at home by drawing attention to them. Examples include asking them to wear name tags or identifying them during the service. Don't expect them to return the following week.

Nearly as deadly are efforts meant to express appreciation for attending a service but invading the visitor's home turf. For instance, a pastor or other church representative going to the home of the visitor without being asked to do so is twice as likely to repulse as to impress the person. ] Wrong

---

### TABLE 4.1

### THE EXPERIENCES NONCHURCHED ADULTS WOULD LIKE—AND DISLIKE— IF THEY VISIT A CHURCH

| | Visitor Reaction | |
| Treatment of Visitor by the Church | Like It | Dislike It |
| --- | --- | --- |
| **FAVORABLE PRACTICES:** | | |
| Nothing special during service; treated no differently | 80% | 13% |
| Greeted individually after the service by people | 78 | 17 |
| Information about the church was made available | 70 | 22 |
| Received a thank-you note from the pastor that week | 70 | 23 |
| Voluntary, church-sponsored reception after the service | 65 | 25 |
| | | |
| **UNFAVORABLE PRACTICES:** | | |
| Pastor or church person visited your home that week | 32 | 64 |
| Asked to wear a name tag at the service | 26 | 65 |
| Asked to identify yourself, as a visitor, during service | 22 | 72 |
| Small gift brought to home as a thank-you for visiting | 21 | 72 |

Similarly, taking a gift to the person as a welcome or thank-you for attending is three times more likely to infuriate as to encourage that person. The most appealing means of showing gratitude for the visit is for the pastor to mail a letter of thanks within a week of the visit. Seven out of 10 nonchurched adults said they would like that approach.

The gist of these messages is that the nonchurched take a big step when they decide to evaluate a church. The last thing they want is pressure put on them by well-intentioned but misinformed church people.

The person who has the greatest opportunity to express the genuine care

■ ■

OUR PROJECTIONS SUGGEST THAT DURING THE COMING YEAR OR SO, ROUGHLY 7 PER-CENT OF THE NONCHURCHED POPULATION WILL SAMPLE A CHURCH.

■ ■ ■

and gratitude of the congregation is the one who invited the visitor to attend. Not only does that person have an easy entrée to the guest, but also a considerable degree of credibility, which will enhance any positive expressions toward the visitor.

Using impersonal and mass-marketing techniques to demonstrate the personal care and individual interest of the church simply does not work in this age of personalized marketing and consumer skepticism.

## THE PROSPECTS

Back in the mid-1980s, the news was encouraging. We noted that up to 40 percent of the nonchurched population would likely return to a Christian church in the near future to evaluate the potential value of a church in their lives. That prediction came to fruition, too, as boomers returned to the church in record numbers.

The period of "easy pickings," however, is past. Today, the ranks of those likely to return to the Christian church in the near future is considerably smaller, and much more finicky. Our projections suggest that during the coming year or so, roughly 7 percent of the nonchurched population will sample a church. Another one-third of the base would consider returning under the right circumstances. Six out of 10 nonchurched adults, however, are unlikely to return.

This news can be seen with optimism or pessimism, depending on your viewpoint. From the optimistic side, if 7 percent return to evaluate churches, that represents more than 5 million men, women and children gracing Christian churches with their presence. That is a huge number of people and a tremendous opportunity to influence many lives with the love and message of Jesus Christ.

Knowing that this is a real possibility should motivate us to prepare immediately for such a substantial test. If you need further motivation to be truly prepared for this potential visitation by the unreached, realize that they do not go from church to church, aggressively searching for the right church home. Whatever brings them back to a church, remember that most of them have had experience in the church and consciously chose to reject it.

If they return to a church—yours—and find that it has little of value to offer, the chances of them trying another church are remote. Worse, the chances of them returning to a Christian church at some point in the future also are severely reduced by their unexceptional experience with the church during this reexamination phase.

Pessimistically speaking, most of the nonchurched people in our nation have rejected the church for the long haul. It is going to take something radical to bring them back to the church—some special move of God, through His people, to influence the unconvinced for His glory. This is not outside the realm of possibility, of course, but it would be outside the natural course of events.

## STRATEGIC EVANGELISM

Armed with such insights about the nonchurched population, the question for you to address is this: How can you design outreach strategies and tactics that reflect a genuine love and concern for the nonchurched, non-Christian people; how can you respond to the idiosyncrasies and perspectives of these people and provide them with a fulfilling and appealing experience that does not compromise the gospel?

As a word of encouragement, realize that the Bible goes to great lengths to speak to the message, the messenger and the motives for reaching out to non-Christian people. But the Bible does not provide any absolute dictums regarding the methods by which we are to reach those people! All you need to know is that you are called to reach them. God wants to bless your efforts to reach them. And what has worked for our church in the past, in a different cultural context, may no longer be effective. We must use the creative and strategic abilities God has invested within us to pursue the souls of those who so desperately need to know God in an intimate, personal, life-changing way.

NOTE

1. We discovered, through our interviews with the nonchurched, that each of the following approaches to communicating would make them less likely to attend a church: a pastor or member of a church visiting their home to talk about the church and to offer an invitation to attend; exposure to media advertising on behalf of the church; receiving a telephone call from someone in the community who described the church and invited them to attend; billboard advertising promoting the church; and interaction with a survey taker who visited their home, asked questions about church attendance and interests, then invited the respondent to attend the survey taker's church. Only two items were found to have a positive effect on people's likelihood of attending a church: being invited by a trusted friend or attending interesting and top-quality events sponsored by the church. A direct-mail approach has brought mixed results.

# 5

# EVANGELISM
# IN ACTION

Every day, thousands of Americans accept Jesus Christ as their Savior. This is no small miracle because such a decision swims against the tide of individualism and self-importance that is flooding the nation. It is a decision that does not just happen without provocation or a serious motivation. It occurs because people like you and me take the time to build relationships with nonbelievers, demonstrate the power and love of Christ in our own lives and do whatever is rational and necessary to facilitate those people making the decision to follow Christ.

If you were to take the secular media reports at face value, you might conclude that evangelism is ancient history: People are scared to do it, nonbelievers are annoyed by it, the process no longer works and once Billy Graham passes from the evangelistic scene there may never be another like him.

## THE PERSONAL TOUCH

Thankfully, the impressions delivered by the media are grossly inaccurate. To correct the erroneous perceptions, consider these research findings:

- Interpersonal evangelism is alive and evident. During the past year, more than 60 million adults (one-third of the adult population) claim to have shared their religious beliefs with someone they felt had different religious beliefs in the hope that the recipient might accept Jesus Christ as personal Savior.
- The people who share their faith with nonbelievers do so often. On average, lay evangelists share with one person every month. Projected through the course of a year, this suggests that nearly

three-quarters of a billion evangelistic conversations take place each year in America.

To get the complete picture, however, you must add to this the exposure of TV viewers to evangelistic pitches made by people such as Billy Graham, Charles Stanley, Pat Robertson and others; invitations to accept Christ that are heard through Christian radio programming; the millions of pieces of evangelistic literature that are distributed; Christian books that are written for the purpose of leading a person to accept Christ as personal Savior; Christian songs that are played on the airwaves and Christian videos that are watched on TV; and the numerous evangelistic sermons and invitations at church services and other events.

The bottom line is that more than one billion evangelistic invitations are shared every year in America. If it were possible to accurately count the number of evangelistic exposures made through this vast array of communication methods, it likely would exceed 3 billion in the United States.

- Although it is true that nearly half of all adults indicate they become annoyed when someone tries to share religious beliefs with them, we also have discovered that when those same annoyed individuals have an evangelistic conversation with a family member, close friend or trusted associate, they are not annoyed. Depending upon the state of mind or point of spiritual quest of the nonbeliever, the person may even express gratitude for the interest shown in them.

- Much of evangelism fails to result in conversions. The task of the Christian, however, is to be faithful in sharing the gospel. It is the job of the Holy Spirit to complete the process by leading the nonbeliever to decide to follow Christ. Success in evangelism is obedience to the call to evangelize, not the number of conversions in which a person plays a part.

- Billy Graham has been one of the great evangelists in world history. God has used him mightily throughout the world for four decades. To suggest, however, that the era of evangelism will close with his retirement is like suggesting that no more churches would be planted after the death of the apostle Paul. God does not rely upon one single person.

Today, more than 3,000 people serve as itinerant evangelists, much as Dr. Graham has served. They use a variety of methods to bring the gospel to the people, ranging from massive crusades to one-on-one conversations, and are living proof that evangelism will continue well into the next century.

- Every year, approximately 1 million people receive some kind of evangelism training. In most cases, this consists of classes or other preparation provided by their churches. In other situations, this equipping occurs in classes at schools and seminaries, in seminars and conferences on evangelistic activity, in personal mentoring and in training offered by parachurch ministries such as Evangelism Explosion, Campus Crusade for Christ and the Billy Graham Evangelistic Association. Overall, among the 60 million adults who shared their faith with non-Christians last year, almost half of them (47 percent) have had some form of evangelism training during their lifetimes.

These are encouraging signs. As long as believers in America are devoted to bringing others to faith in Christ by using all possible means at their disposal, there is hope for the nation. And yet, although millions of Christians share their faith with nonbelievers, much is still to be done. We can learn a lot about how to complete the task of evangelizing America by understanding those people who are engaged in evangelism, the opportunities yet to be exploited and the approaches and strategies that seem to produce the most positive results.

## ATTRIBUTES OF AN EVANGELIZER

In a nationwide survey we recently conducted among the people who have shared their beliefs with non-Christians during the past year, we discovered that little distinguishes them from the total Christian population. This insight should serve as an encouragement to each of us. To understand why, consider what we now know about Christians who evangelize their world.

We found, for example, that most Christians who evangelize do not claim to have the spiritual gift of evangelism. Only one out of every eight (12 percent) said he or she had this special gift for outreach. The vast majority of those who share their faith either said that they do not have this gift or do not know what their gifts are. The focus they maintain is on God's calling to each of us to be His witnesses in the world whenever they have opportunities to be such ambassadors of faith.

We also discovered that these evangelizers do not have any special qualifications that have pushed them to the front lines of the evangelistic war zone. An examination of the demographic profile of the evangelistic corps shows that this group has the same median age as the national population and the same proportion are married and have children in their households. They are similar in their ethnic composure to the aggregate population.

Their median household income levels are equivalent to the national average.

The only noteworthy differences are that evangelizers are somewhat more likely than the norm to be women, to live outside of the Northeastern states, to have completed a college education and to be conservative politically. The Bible tells us that every person who believes in Christ as Savior is called to share the good news (see Matt. 28:18-20; John 14:12; Acts 1:8; 1 Cor. 11:1). Research tells us that people from all walks of life and a variety of backgrounds are sharing that good news.

When we assess the church affiliations of evangelizers, we find they have been strategically placed by God in every imaginable place of Christian worship Once again, the research shows no huge differences between the denominational preferences of churchgoers and those people who spread the good news. People attending evangelical and charismatic or Pentecostal churches have a slightly higher tendency to be involved in spreading their spiritual joy to others. The real story, however, is that we see evangelizers in every denomination, in churches of all sizes and in churches of all theological and doctrinal stripes.

## THE HEART OF AN EVANGELIZER

Perhaps the most distinguishing characteristics are the hearts of those who put their relationships, reputations and resources on the line to inform other people about salvation through grace made available through Jesus Christ.

When we think of courage, we conjure images of brave military leaders who participate in daring escapades in battle. We may wish to alter our image of courage, however, to encompass the hundreds of thousands of Christians who dare to tell others that meaning, purpose, success, peace and joy in life are not derived from material or relational pleasures, but from a vibrant and growing relationship with Jesus Christ.

According to the evangelizers, only half of them were aware that any of the people they had ever shared with made a decision to follow Jesus. Yet, they continue to promote the gospel without regard to the outcome.

This can play both ways, of course. Continued rejection of the gospel might be a sign that the manner in which the person is sharing is ineffective and needs to be changed. On the other hand, if conversion is truly the domain of the Holy Spirit, then only so much can be expected of a person who is trying to faithfully and articulately spread the message of hope through faith in Christ.

Many evangelizers are realistic about their efforts to serve God through their witness of His offer of salvation. One-quarter of them admitted they could have done a better job if they had tried harder or had thought their efforts through beforehand.

Three out of every 10 people expressed disappointment in themselves for not having done a better job of sharing their faith. But the fundamental perspective that drives evangelizers is that God is in control and can make the best of even the least proficient effort.

More than 9 out of 10 evangelizers believed that in spite of their own frailties and inadequacies, the mere act of sharing the gospel might have planted crucial ideas in the mind or heart of the nonbeliever. An even greater proportion (97 percent) thought it had been a privilege to tell their counterpart about Christ, and that in His own way, in His perfect timing, God would make the most of that encounter.

## ALWAYS BE PREPARED

One of the important lessons derived from our conversations with those engaged in evangelism is that preparation is a key to effectiveness—a perspective confirmed by the Bible (see 1 Pet. 3:15,16).

Almost 9 out of 10 people who shared the gospel (85 percent) said they would like to have been better prepared. The significance of such prepared-

■ ■

THE BURDEN FOR SUCCESS RESTS ON THE HOLY SPIRIT. THE PRIMARY CHALLENGE TO THE BELIEVER IS TO FOLLOW GOD'S LEADING.

■ ■ ■

ness was underscored by the fact that 9 out of 10 evangelizers (91 percent) said they generally wind up sharing their faith with nonbelievers unexpectedly in response to concerns or interests raised in the normal course of conversation rather than as part of a planned evangelistic moment.

The importance of this finding cannot be overstated. Americans like to plan and control matters. But evangelism is not a matter within our control. We may plan when to share the gospel, but frequently the evangelizers found that their plans went awry. When spiritual opportunity knocks, the evangelizer must be ready to address the opportunity, whether it is on the day's schedule or not. As many of the faithful noted, sometimes you only get one good chance to share the ultimate truth with a nonbeliever. You have to be ready at any moment to make the most of the open doors.

What is especially impressive about the evangelizers is that, for the most part, they were accessible to God for the moment of opportunity. Perhaps earlier in this chapter you were surprised, as I was, by the average number of times the typical evangelizer shares the gospel during the course of the year. The reason is likely because God has found these people to be ready and willing to go for it when they have the chance. This availability speaks to the fact that evangelizers recognize that they are merely conduits through which the message is delivered. The burden for success rests on the Holy Spirit. The primary challenge to the believer is to follow God's leading (see John 15:5).

The fact remains, however, that people who are available and thankful for opportunities to spread the good news want to be better prepared to take advantage of outreach opportunities. How can they accomplish this end?

Nine out of 10 evangelizers said they would like to know more about the content of the Bible and 3 out of every 4 suggested that they would like to have a greater number of close friends with whom they could share the good news. These two simple but challenging steps would undoubtedly enhance the ability to make the gospel come alive for many more of those who engage in conversation about what Christ has to offer.

## HOW TO PREPARE

Perhaps you, or maybe other people in your church, are in the same situation. You would like to be an effective evangelizer but you need more ammunition. How can you get ready for the opportunities that might present themselves at any moment?

If the experience of the existing cadre of evangelizers provides insight, then taking the initiative is critical. Part of the task of an evangelizer is to take the necessary steps to be ready to spontaneously share the Word of God with those in need (see 2 Tim. 4:2).

Most evangelizers have prepared for evangelizing opportunities by enrolling in training courses. In most cases, this was education made available through their churches. We also found, however, that only one out of every three Christian churches offers evangelism training. If that avenue is closed, you can turn to myriad parachurch organizations that provide opportunities to learn about people. You can also turn to the Bible and to communication and evangelism techniques and strategies that teach how to develop friendships that may blossom into opportunities to share.

Part of the motivation for training is to compensate or to prepare for some of the challenges that evangelizers typically face. For instance, we discovered:

√ Four out of 10 evangelizers are usually concerned that they will not do a good job of clearly explaining their beliefs.

√ One out of every three Christians who shares his or her faith enters the discussion with concerns about a personal lack of knowledge and skill in answering the questions these people might ask regarding Christianity.

√ Three out of 10 evangelizers are usually worried that the person they are evangelizing will be upset or offended by the nature of the discussion.

√ One out of every seven feels uncomfortable speaking with other people about spiritual matters.

Why do those who promote the gospel take the risk of experiencing these difficulties? Partially because they have reached a stage in their relationship with Christ at which they are excited about having a chance to tell someone else about the miraculous work of Christ. Further, 9 out of 10 have lofty expectations, believing that God will bless their efforts, whether the person exposed to the gospel presentation invites Christ to be their Savior or not.

Knowing that they are obeying God's call to share, that Christ will be honored by their efforts to evangelize, that the Holy Spirit will complete the work and that the person who is hearing the gospel has the potential to lead a fully transformed life should he or she decide to embrace Christ, the specter of failure, insensitivity, personal inadequacy or discomfort pale in comparison to the privilege of taking part in the process and the product of evangelizing.

## HOW PEOPLE SHARE THEIR FAITH

Our research revealed a cornerstone principle: There is no "right" way to introduce other people to Christ. The experience of the evangelizers shows that many approaches can be used, and each may be appropriate for a certain circumstance, a certain kind of evangelizer or for a certain kind of nonbeliever.

In general, we learned that four out of five evangelizers promote the benefits of being a Christian (79 percent); three-quarters of the evangelizers involve their nonbelieving counterpart in the process by asking them questions about their beliefs and life experiences (75 percent); most Christians tell their personal story of how they came to accept Christ as their Savior (59 percent); most usually quote passages from the Bible to make their case (58 percent); and about half spend time praying for the specific person and for a profitable time of sharing before getting together and discussing spiritual truths (54 percent).

One of the true keys to effective evangelism is prayer. Six out of 10 evangelizers say they have targeted certain people and consistently pray for their salvation. Notice, too, that in comparison to those who share the gospel but do not pray for people beforehand, those who pray for the souls of specific people are more than 30 percent more likely to have seen people accept Christ as their Savior after sharing the gospel with them.

## FIVE METHODS OF EVANGELISM USED TODAY

Five dominant approaches to personal evangelism appear to be in common use today. From most common to least common, these methods are as follows:

### LIFESTYLE OR FRIENDSHIP EVANGELISM

Besides being the most common form of personal evangelism (used by 79 percent of all laity involved in evangelism), this is perhaps the most loosely defined or structured approach as well. Lifestyle evangelism is often criticized because it is a "soft sell" strategy that takes time for the gospel to be firmly explained to the nonbeliever.

The distinguishing characteristic of this approach is that it is based on developing significant, credible relationships with nonbelievers. The foundation of this approach is that you build an authentic, nonmanipulative relationship with a nonbeliever, reflect a lifestyle that is overtly but not offensively different from the norm, raise the curiosity of the nonbeliever through such idiosyncratic behavior and have the opportunity at the request of the nonbeliever to describe the reasons and motivations underlying your unique way of life.

Joe Aldrich describes lifestyle evangelism as a three-step procedure. First, you must have a significant presence in the life of the non-Christian. Before the nonbeliever will listen to the gospel, he or she must feel the love on which the gospel is allegedly based.

Second, you must proclaim the gospel verbally. No matter how intriguing your disparate lifestyle might be, the underlying reasons will not become clear to the nonbeliever, and he or she will not have a real chance to embrace Christ as a result of your efforts, unless your faith in Christ is explained.

Third, the person may be persuaded to accept Christ—that is, to make a "decision for Christ"—if the prior two steps seem real and the prospects of being Christian seem worthwhile.[1]

Aldrich states that the major advantages of lifestyle evangelism are that it puts minimal pressure on the evangelizer, it demands limited scriptural knowledge because the focus is on who the believer is and how he or she became so different, and the appropriate time to share is determined by the nonbeliever rather than the believer.

The primary disadvantage of this lifestyle evangelism approach is that it can become an easy excuse for Christians. Instead of diligently and aggressively pursuing evangelistic opportunities, Christians may easily convince themselves that if they just lead good lives, are friendly and open to sharing their faith, God will take care of the rest.

Effective lifestyle evangelizers, however, are more aggressive in their selection of friends and in identifying nonbelievers with whom they relate comfortably and whose presence they enjoy. Indeed, our surveys indicated that lifestyle evangelism is the most common approach among evangelizers and is especially popular among those who share their faith least often and who are least likely to know of anyone accepting Christ as Savior through the efforts of the evangelizer.

## FAMILY EVANGELISM

This is the approach in which one family member will share the gospel with another family member. For a majority of Christian adults, this is the only people group they will ever attempt to evangelize. Family evangelism is similar to lifestyle evangelism in that it is based on relational trust and intimacy. It differs in that it generally does not rely upon the inquiries of a family member to initiate the conversation that leads to a verbal proclamation of the gospel.

The believer usually takes the initiative in these circumstances and seeks to persuade the nonbelieving family member of the importance of a decision for Christ. Because of the deeper emotional bonds involved in family sharing and because the believer tends to initiate the conversation, family evangelism results in heated discussions, hurt feelings and broken relationships more often than in lifestyle outreach efforts. Roughly one-quarter of all adults engage in this manner of outreach to loved ones.

## CONFRONTATIONAL EVANGELISM

This is the classic, traditional form of evangelism in which Christians meet a person they probably do not know and share the good news. Sometimes, of course, confrontational evangelism occurs among people known to the evangelizer, such as work associates or neighbors, with whom the Christian does not have a particularly strong or long relationship.

The distinguishing attribute of this strategy is that the Christian usually determines who is exposed to the gospel, when and where the exposure takes place and is typically dogmatic about having the hearer make a decision on the spot or risk eternal condemnation.

The settings in which such encounters occur are innumerable: in the nonbeliever's home (e.g., door-to-door, cold-call evangelism); at places of leisure activity (e.g., the beach, at concerts); in public places (e.g., on buses or airplanes, in parking lots of sporting events); or in virtually any imaginable place where two people might hold a conversation. Street-corner evangelists have become the stereotypical purveyors of this method. Numerically, however, street evangelism is among the least common forms of confrontational outreach.

### CELL-GROUP EVANGELISM

Cell-group evangelism is one of the most frequently talked about strategies in the marketplace today. Approximately 3 percent of all adults are involved in any kind of cell group in which evangelism is one of the foci of the meeting. Cell groups are essentially small groups of people who meet regularly for some form of Christian activity. Most small groups revolve around teaching, prayer and building interpersonal relationships. Most groups meet one weeknight each week or every other week for about 90 minutes. The participants are usually Christians who are active in a local church from which the group originates.

The notion of cell-group evangelism is to develop a comfortable setting in which nonbelievers are welcomed and feel at ease. During the course of the evening, people discuss the Christian faith and what it means to them, how they can grow in their faith and perhaps how others in the group might help them in that growth. At an appropriate time during the meeting, participants have an opportunity to declare their desire to commit their lives to Christ if they have not already done so. This process can be handled with varying degrees of sensitivity.

The design of the group also varies—some are ongoing groups of believers who seek to invite, involve and evangelize nonbelievers. Others are short-term groups whose primary purpose is to address specific social or spiritual issues in which non-Christians may have an interest. Their intent may be to address existing concerns and questions and then invite the nonbelievers to accept Christ.

### POWER EVANGELISM

Power evangelism is probably the most controversial of the most common personal evangelism techniques. This approach is much more common outside the United States. Power evangelism is based on the contention that when Jesus and the disciples ministered, they sought converts through two acts.

First, they proclaimed the gospel verbally. Second, they demonstrated the power of God through acts of love or service (e.g., healing). Those who advocate power evangelism suggest that this is a combination of the rational with the transrational. Instead of relying solely upon an intellectual assent to spiritual truths and principles, this strategy offers the nonbeliever a physical demonstration of the power of the gospel.

Currently, about 3 percent of American adults engage in some form of power evangelism. Popularized in America through the work of John Wimber and the Vineyard Christian Fellowship congregations, the use of the charismatic gifts to "authenticate the gospel" has made this a hotly debated approach.[2] Its proponents argue that the use of the gifts to produce miracles draws focused attention to the message of the gospel and the power of God, thereby reducing resistance to the perceived limitations of Christianity in the American context.

## CORPORATE OUTREACH

Not all evangelism is conducted on a one-to-one basis, though. A substantial degree of outreach aimed at saving the nonbelievers is conducted by ministry organizations. Interestingly, although personal evangelistic efforts represent the most prolific number of evangelistic exposures, corporate evangelistic activity consumes a much greater amount of money.

Not including the money spent by churches on their weekend services, several billion dollars every year are designated for domestic evangelistic activity. This spending underwrites a host of activities ranging from televised crusades to literature campaigns, parachurch-sponsored social welfare programs to church planting.

The most traditional evangelistic activities initiated by ministry organizations include media evangelism such as television, radio and literature outreach efforts; evangelistic crusades such as those by Billy Graham, Luis Palau, Greg Laurie and Steve Russo; special evangelistic meetings of various sorts, featuring the ministry of itinerant evangelists; social welfare programs such as the work of the Salvation Army, Habitat for Humanity or Prison Fellowship; confrontational evangelism conducted by organizations as varied as Campus Crusade for Christ (and its three dozen subsidiary ministries), Full Gospel Business Men's Fellowship and Jews for Jesus; and youth rallies and events (Youth for Christ, Young Life and Pioneer Clubs are among the best known).

Many event-oriented activities often are overlooked by people who discuss evangelism but they account for a significant number of evangelistic contacts and decisions for Christ. Among the most significant are concerts designed for evangelistic purposes, such as those by contemporary Christian artists, including Michael W. Smith, Petra, DeGarmo & Key, Steven Curtis

Chapman and DC Talk; dramatic presentations by drama troupes (e.g., Lamb's Players) or individual dramatic performers; and sports ministries that seek to reach the non-Christian world (e.g., Athletes in Action).

## CORPORATE INNOVATION

In terms of the most recent and innovative evangelistic methods that deserve special mention, we might focus upon church planting and prayer evangelism. C. Peter Wagner, the dean of what is known as the "church growth movement," has called the birthing of new churches the most significant evangelistic method on the horizon. Three decades of research on Christianity has led him to conclude, "The single most effective evangelistic methodology under heaven is planting new churches."[3]

■ ■

PRAYER EVANGELISM IS A STRATEGY FOR URBAN EVANGELISM, AND GIVEN THAT 76 PERCENT OF AMERICA'S POPULATION LIVES IN METROPOLITAN AREAS, AN URBAN EMPHASIS IS WARRANTED.

■ ■ ■

Wagner goes on to detail why church planting is such an effective means of reaching nonbelievers, citing the following reasons:

- New leaders are released to use their skills and gifts more effectively than would have been possible in their old churches.
- A new church renews the energy and enthusiasm of some of the existing churches located in the same community.
- A new church has fewer psychological barriers to overcome in developing means of effectively reaching the new generation of adults.
- Numerical growth "is more likely with less effort in new churches" than is likely in older congregations.
- New churches offer unchurched people a wider variety of alternatives to choose from, enhancing their likelihood of attending any church.[4]

If Dr. Wagner is correct, then the late '90s and the early years of the approaching decade should be a boom time for evangelism. Denominations across the nation have committed millions of dollars and hundreds of pastors and staff people to plant new churches.

At one point, our research showed that Protestant denominations and independent churches cumulatively had set plans in motion to establish nearly 75,000 new churches between 1990 and 2010. Given that slightly fewer than 300,000 churches were in existence at the time, this represents a phenomenal commitment to increasing the base of churches—and, ostensibly—to evangelism.

Another recent foray into the evangelistic frontier has been the prayer evangelism movement. This has been documented in the writing of Dr. Wagner and in that of Joe Aldrich, David Bryant and Ed Silvoso.[5] Prayer evangelism is a strategy for urban evangelism, and given that 76 percent of America's population lives in metropolitan areas, an urban emphasis is warranted.

The typical strategy of the prayer evangelism approach is to develop prayer cells throughout a target city so that every home and neighborhood are being prayed for daily. The strategy incorporates warfare prayer principles and is founded upon the coordinated efforts of as many churches as possible from within the target geography. Often, the united church effort is preceded by a time of repentant prayer in which the division and disunity among the churches is jointly repudiated by church leaders.

Strategically, the churches then come together to establish the geographic perimeter of their prayer and evangelistic activity; to secure that perimeter by rooting out any discernible disunity, apathy and spiritual ignorance within the church camp; to infiltrate the perimeter of the enemy (i.e., Satan), a task accomplished through warfare prayer; and to take back the city for Christ.

Such prayer evangelism campaigns have been launched in many cities in nations around the world and have proven wildly successful. They are just beginning to take shape in America and will be one of the more visible and unusual means of winning people to Christ during the next decade and beyond.

## WHAT ABOUT THE LOCAL CHURCH?

In the next chapter, we will examine some of the strategies employed by the most aggressive and evangelistic churches in the nation. But not every church is able to devise creative strategies or mobilize thousands of people for special outreach campaigns. Yet, every church is called to engage in evangelism.

Oddly, the typical church in America is only moderately involved in reaching nonbelievers. Statistics we have gathered for the past two years may help paint the portrait of the evangelistic malaise.

- The average Protestant church spends more money on buildings and maintenance than it does on evangelism. For every dollar devoted to outreach activities, the average church will spend more than five dollars on real estate.
- When asked to identify the primary joys they receive from pastoring, only one-quarter of senior pastors (28 percent) stated that seeing nonbelievers turn their lives over to Christ was at or near the top of the list.
- Only one out of every eight senior pastors (12 percent) strongly agrees that "most Christian adults are capable of effectively sharing their faith with nonbelievers."
- Fewer than half of all senior pastors believe they are doing either an excellent or good job at leading their churches in evangelism.
- When asked to describe their churches, fewer than one out of every four pastors said his church could be described as "evangelistic." In fact, of the 14 attributes examined in the study, this attribute received the lowest rating.
- Seven out of 10 senior pastors claimed that evangelism was to be a top priority for their churches in the coming year, ranking this activity third in a long list of choices.
- In the vast majority of churches, the only full-time minister at the church is the senior pastor. On average, senior pastors devote about two hours each week to activities related to evangelism.
- Only one out of every three churches offers its people any kind of formal evangelism training. In churches that offer training, an average of 10 people are exposed to such equipping during the year. The church will devote approximately $900 from its budget to evangelism training. That represents roughly 1 percent of the aggregate annual budget for ministry.
- The average annual budget allocated by the typical church for all of its local evangelistic endeavors amounts to only about 2 percent of the gross annual revenues received by the church.

In general, we found that churches have an interest in growing numerically but have a very limited commitment to investing in evangelism. Most pastors, having neither the gift of evangelism (only 9 percent of senior pastors claim to have it) nor a driving passion to consistently relate to nonbelievers, do not aggressively push an evangelistic agenda.

Most pastors will, at some time during the year, make public statements in support of evangelism. Few pastors can be accused of outright rejection of evangelism as a church thrust. They support the notion of local evangelism. They applaud the efforts of evangelizers, and they are personally comfortable with discipling new believers.

The vast majority of churches includes one or more evangelistic sermons in weekend services each year. However, pastors who consistently preach with the intention of convincing the non-Christians who might be attending any given service represent a minority. Most pastors preach a few sermons during the year for the purpose of reaching the unreached. And although several thousand churches (again, a distinct minority) have a "pastor of evangelism" on staff, the primary role of these staff members is to motivate, manage and monitor the laity who are already fired up about reaching out to the lost sheep in the community.

Many churches also attempt to sponsor evangelistic events. These range from special dramatic presentations during the major holiday seasons to potluck dinners in the church hall when each member is expected to bring a non-Christian guest or two. Programs such as "Friend Day" are used widely as a means of introducing newcomers to the church with a minimum of effort.

Participation in evangelistic crusades by evangelists is yet another kind of event that is frequently utilized by churches. Our research showed, however, that the typical church believes in evangelism but is not willing to break new ground and take even moderate risks when it comes to local evangelism.

Intriguingly, then, churches are typically not on the cutting edge of evangelism. A small number of churches around the nation focus heavily on evangelism, but they are the exception to the rule.

## THE SEEKER CHURCH

One exception to the notion that most churches are neither on the cutting edge nor willing to be innovative or take risks to penetrate the ranks of the non-Christians is the continued growth of seeker churches.

Initiated by Willow Creek Community Church in South Barrington, Illinois, in the mid-1970s, seeker churches have based their ministries on a philosophy that esteems effective evangelism and designs all of the church's activities and programs around that philosophy. The seeker-church approach has grown from nothing to more than 10,000 churches nationwide.

Bill Hybels, founding pastor of Willow Creek, explains the initiation and development of the seeker style as a response to feeling "called to be difference makers. We wanted to be open to new strategies that would honor God.

"So, after conducting a neighborhood survey to determine why people didn't attend church, Willow Creek created an innovative 'seeker service' with drama, contemporary music and relevant messages," he said.

"Instead of traditional Sunday morning worship services for believers, we plan weekend services targeted to lost people. We challenge and train our believers to invite their nonchurched friends to attend with them. Our typical weekend visitor is 'Unchurched Harry,' who's between 25 and 45 years old."[6]

Some of the assumptions that undergird the seeker church's ministry are the following:

- Every believer has the responsibility of being a witness in one's faith and walk with Christ.
- The needs of a seeker differ from those of a believer.
- Believers must respect the individual's process of a faith decision and the journey one must travel to maturity in Christ.
- Every believer is a minister, gifted by God for the benefit of the Body.[7]

Having this kind of perspective operating as the basis for designing ministry activities and adventures, the seeker church then develops a strategy for outreach, which then results in the grassroots ministry efforts that facilitate the involvement of believers in the lives of nonbelievers.

One of the most popular strategic statements is the seven-step strategy developed by Willow Creek and adopted by hundreds of seeker churches across the nation. The strategy was designed specifically to enable Willow Creek (and its cousins) to accomplish its mission to exalt God, to edify the saints, to evangelize the lost and to engage in social action.

The Willow Creek strategy is certainly not the only plan of action that a seeker church can devise. Thousands of seeker churches have crafted various strategies for a seeker-oriented ministry, but the Willow Creek model has worked well during the two decades the church has been in existence. Willow Creek attracts about 15,000 people to its weekend services, and thousands of people have accepted Christ.

## THE SEVEN-STEP STRATEGY

Here is the seven-step strategy that drives Willow Creek:

1. Believers must build relational bridges to the unchurched.
2. Once those relationships are secure, believers are expected to share their faith with their nonbeliever friends.

3. To capitalize on the nonbeliever's curiosity, the believer may invite the nonbeliever to attend a weekend seeker service, which is meant to support the evangelistic efforts of those who have built relationships with non-Christians.
4. The spiritual needs of the believer are addressed in a midweek service of worship and instruction. Should a nonbeliever accept Christ as Savior, the midweek services supplement what is received from the weekend seeker services.
5. Every believer is expected to participate in a small group of believers that meets during the week for fellowship, accountability, discipleship, encouragement and support.
6. Believers are expected to be involved in ministry, not merely to attend events and to observe the activity of the church. This is a primary outlet for a person's gifts.
7. Believers are called to be good stewards of their resources as an act of discipleship and worship.[8]

As many as one-fifth of all churches claim they now have some kind of seeker service. We found that the definition of a seeker service varies widely, ranging from the radical approach taken by Willow Creek of totally redesigning the church's ministry to highlight the importance of reaching nonbelievers in creative ways, to churches that mix a few praise and worship songs with traditional hymns in the hope of seeming more relevant to non-Christian visitors.

Not surprisingly, seeker churches are most likely to be new churches. It is extremely difficult to transform a traditional-style church into one that intentionally and overtly targets nonbelievers through a dramatic change in its philosophy of ministry, services, staffing, programs, budgeting and outreach efforts.

We also have found various degrees of emphasis upon the "seeker." The most courageous of these churches are "seeker driven," while a much larger proportion of the seeker-oriented congregations are more properly described as "seeker sensitive," meaning they want to be accessible to seekers but not at the expense of the traditions, routines or other believer-driven church activities.

## GRASSROOTS EVANGELISM

More often than not, then, we find that pastors hope and pray that the people of the congregation will take it upon themselves to figure out how to build relationships with those outside the Body of Christ, to determine how to most effectively share the gospel with non-Christians and to do the necessary follow-up to incorporate the new believers into the life of the church.

Far from being a cop-out by pastors, the Bible indicates that this is exactly how evangelism is to be accomplished—through individual people empowered by the Body of believers and its leaders to become unassuming, genuine street-level evangelizers (see Matt. 28:18-20; Acts 1:8; 6:7,8,10; 8:4-8,26-35; 9:10-18; 11:19-21; 1 Pet. 3:15).

But as we search for the cutting edge in evangelism today, another revelation emerges. We find it in the work of parachurch ministries where a passion for evangelism is at the heart of the organization and the idiosyncratic efforts of individual evangelizers.

NOTES

1. Joseph Aldrich, *Life-Style Evangelism* (Portland, Ore.: Multnomah Press, 1981), pp. 81-84.
2. John Wimber and Kevin Springer, *Power Evangelism* (San Francisco: HarperSanFrancisco, 1985; reprint, 1992), p. xx.
3. C. Peter Wagner, *Church Planting for a Greater Harvest* (Ventura, Calif.: Regal Books, 1990), p. 11.
4. Ibid., pp. 19-37.
5. For more information about the prayer evangelism movement, see Ed Silvoso, *That None Should Perish* (Ventura, Calif.: Regal Books, 1994); C. Peter Wagner, *Prayer Shield* (Ventura, Calif.: Regal Books, 1992); C. Peter Wagner, ed., *Breaking Strongholds in Your City* (Ventura, Calif.: Regal Books, 1993).
6. *Willow Creek Community Church—Church Leaders Handbook* (South Barrington, Ill.: Willow Creek Community Church, 1991), p. v.
7. Ibid., p. 4.
8. Ibid., pp. 4-5.

# 6

# CHURCHES ON
# THE EDGE

Among the 300,000 Protestant churches in America, we estimate that more than 85 percent of them have a mission, purpose, vision or goals statement that acknowledges the need and commitment to evangelize. Yet, our research also suggests that a relatively small minority of those congregations are truly driven to fulfill that mandate.

Evangelism is a paradox. Almost every church leader assents to the importance of evangelism and a desire to have a church that takes the promotion of the gospel seriously. But a comparative handful of those churches carry out their stated evangelistic intention with true passion, urgency, diligence and joy.

Clearly, something different stimulates the truly evangelistically minded churches to focus on intentionally, intelligently and persistently sharing the gospel.[1] Through a special research project we conducted among churches that are recognized by pastors and denominational leaders to be truly evangelistic in nature, we have identified some of the distinguishing characteristics of the leading evangelistic churches. Along the way, we also encountered a few surprises that may amuse, shock or confuse you.[2]

## THE EVANGELISTIC IMPULSE

In the American context, the natural tendency is to emphasize aspects of ministry other than evangelism, such as worship, discipleship or social welfare activities. Churches that place evangelism at the top of the priorities list are unique. I believe three major reasons explain this tendency.

First, our research discovered that in almost every case, *the driving force behind an evangelistic ministry was the intense desire of the senior pastor to emphasize evangelism.* The following are expressions that pastors, staff members and congregants used to describe the importance of the senior pastor's passion for reaching the unreached:

- "It is the single most important reason we are evangelistic."
- "It is totally important; evangelism is his heartbeat."
- "That's the key; he has a heart for souls and a passion to see lost people saved."
- "It's of supreme importance here; evangelism is his heartbeat; it's his vision."
- "It's everything; it's 100 percent of the reason why we are so driven evangelistically."
- "It is the core; it simply wouldn't happen without it"
- "It's extremely important; he sets the values and the vision for us."
- "No question, that is absolutely indispensable; through his leadership, his passion, his example, he defines us."
- "He is the pacesetter; his emphasis on evangelism will make or break the church's willingness to buy into it."[3]

Interviewing the pastors of the most successful evangelistic churches is nothing short of fascinating. You can fire questions at them about budgets, organizational structures, staff development and program expansion, and they can answer with precision and insight.

Ask the pastors about the evangelistic heart and agenda of the church and you are suddenly speaking to new people. Their enthusiasm and commitment regarding evangelism is obvious and contagious. It would be virtually impossible to work for such a pastor, or to last long in a church led by him, without sharing the same enthusiasm for reaching the unreached.

It occurred to me that in our work with secular organizations, the leader shapes the heart and passion of the corporate entity. In our work with nonprofit organizations, we have found the same principle to be operative. When it comes to the focus of the organization, the people who serve there tend to take on many of the core personality traits of the leader toward fulfilling the mandate of the organization. If this is true, and most churches seem to lack fervor and focus for evangelism, is it reasonable to conclude that it may be because of the lack of zeal most pastors have for identifying, befriending, loving and evangelizing non-Christian people?

A second shaping factor is that each of these churches is *marked by a philosophy of ministry in which evangelism is the centerpiece.* The church's philosophy of ministry statement or document typically encompasses a wide range of factors that determine what the church believes, how it operates and what goals and objectives drive the ministry. The corporate personality and culture and the ministry programs of the church are the tangible product of this statement.

## PHILOSOPHY OF MINISTRY

Many churches have developed a philosophy of ministry. The following three issues seem to differentiate the philosophies of evangelistic churches from those of most other Christian churches in the United States.

*1. Every person is an evangelistic agent.* Most churches use vague language regarding who is responsible for involvement in evangelistic activity.

The unspoken assumption seems to be that evangelism happens mostly

■ ■

## EVERY CHRISTIAN IS CALLED TO INCORPO-RATE AN EVANGELISTIC ASPECT TO HIS OR HER MINISTRY EFFORTS, REGARDLESS OF INDIVIDUAL GIFTS AND ABILITIES.

■ ■ ■

at the weekend services held at the church building, usually in response to the preaching or other pastor-driven efforts that transpire during the service. In contrast, the statements developed by most of the leading evangelistic churches contain no ambiguity about what drives the process—it is neither the institutional church nor the corporate gathering experience, but the individual Christian who is an active member of the local Body.

Every person who calls that church his or her spiritual home is expected to behave as an evangelist, which generally infers building genuine, non-manipulative relationships with non-Christians and working through various means or opportunities to facilitate a conversion in the life of the non-believer.

*2. Evangelism is a lifestyle, not a program.* Most churches have organized an evangelism committee or perhaps an evangelism ministry or team. These are the people who are passionate about reaching the unreached, and they operate as a unit responsible for engaging in evangelistic activity.

In the leading evangelistic churches, however, evangelism is not an isolated activity separated from other ministry or personal growth endeavors. It is expected that every ministry, event, program, department and service will fully integrate evangelism into its efforts. The foundational perspective is that ministry must be viewed holistically.[4]

Consequently, evangelism cannot be separated from any of the other critical functions of ministry and of the family of faith. Every Christian is called to be a minister. Every Christian is called to incorporate an evangelistic aspect to his or her ministry efforts, regardless of individual gifts and abilities or the primary focus of personal ministry efforts.

*3. Evangelistic success is defined differently.* In many of the less evangelistic churches, success is defined by the number of people who attend the church or by the number of nonbelievers who make a decision to follow Christ as their Lord and Savior in response to the church or its people sharing the gospel.

The cutting-edge evangelistic churches have a different slant. Their definition of success in evangelism is that the people active in the church are intentionally and obediently sharing their faith with nonbelievers.

The outcome of sharing is insignificant in determining the success of the person's ministry because the decision made by the nonbeliever is beyond the control of the evangelizer. In most cases, the evangelistic church also looks upon personal follow-up by the evangelizer with the evangelized as a vital part of the process.

The senior pastor often serves as the catalyst for developing the philosophy of ministry, even if staff, committees and other groups of people are involved in the process.

We also discovered that sometimes the evangelistic agenda of the church revolves around the directives of the pastor rather than through widespread exposure and deference to his thoughts expressed in a position paper. This was particularly true of the black and Pentecostal evangelistic churches we studied. In other words, those churches have a philosophy of ministry that has been developed and articulated, but it is shared orally and through common ministry behaviors rather than in writing.

The third defining influence is that *the staff and congregation "own" the mission or vision for ministry, which is largely focused upon local outreach.* If the senior pastor were to be evangelistically inclined and to single-handedly push the outreach ministry, the church would not be known as an evangelistic beacon.

These churches have gained their reputation and have proven the validity of that image by working as a congregation to punch holes in the spiritual darkness that resides in their midst. Among the core roles of the senior pastor are to challenge the congregation to embrace an evangelistic-oriented mission, to enable the people to understand and embrace that perspective as a part of their personal lifestyles and to continually keep the congregation focused upon the things that matter most in ministry.

The ability of evangelistic church pastors to gain widespread ownership of a vision or mission anchored on evangelism is a testimony to their personal passion for evangelism, their ability as leaders and their persistence in positioning a culturally unpopular activity as a congregationally embraced perspective and lifestyle.

# COMMON CHARACTERISTICS OF EVANGELISTIC CHURCHES

Our investigation of what makes evangelistic churches tick also uncovered six traits these churches all had in common. It may be possible to have an evangelistic church without possessing each of these characteristics, but we did not find any that broke this mold.

*1. The weekend services are central to winning souls.* The teaching, preaching and stated philosophies of these churches do not position the Saturday or Sunday church services as central to the evangelistic harvest reaped by the congregation.

Upon evaluating the strategies and activities of these churches, however, it is clear that pastors continue to view the services as the focal point of the church's evangelistic activities. Relationships that develop between believers and nonbelievers are generally seen as the precursor to inviting nonbelievers to the church service where they will be exposed to the presence of God in various forms (worship, teaching, fellowship), which may facilitate decisions to follow Christ.

None of the pastors we interviewed rejected the possibility that the relationships developed by church participants with non-believers would result in conversions outside of the church services. These pastors, however, do not focus their attention on venues other than church services when thinking about the greatest potential for a plentiful harvest of souls.

Although nonbelievers may accept Christ through some other avenue (e.g., an evangelistic event or a personal witnessing incident), it is the new believer's appearance at the church service that is latently thought to confirm the decision and that leads to the ability to "count" the decision through baptism, enrollment in a follow-up class or some other personal investment in personal spiritual growth.

Thus, events and other activities are typically seen as "preevangelistic" efforts. More often than not, it is assumed that the events will "soften" the person's heart for a clear and contextualized presentation of the gospel. The associated assumption is that during the weekend church service the pastor's message and associated opportunities to make a decision to follow Christ will bear spiritual fruit; that is, the church's services are considered to be the major harvesting mechanism.

*2. The ministry focus of the congregation is constantly directed to local outreach.* One of the most appealing characteristics of these churches is the presence of an intentional, concerted and consistent effort to keep the congregation focused on and involved in evangelistic activity. The pastors of these churches recognize that evangelism, even when it is a core value of the congregation, can easily become an "out-of-sight, out-of-mind" element because of so many other ministry options vying for each person's resources.

To combat the onslaught of ministry clutter and resulting diversions while maintaining an environment in which evangelism remains primary, the church typically uses a multitude of tools and mechanisms. Among the most common tactics are the following:

- Sermons and other forms of teaching that relate to the necessity and means of Christians sharing their faith;
- Use of communication tools such as newsletters, pastoral letters and brochures promoting service opportunities;
- Highlighting outreach events as major evangelistic opportunities;
- Offering a substantial number of instructional and training opportunities related to personal evangelism;
- Having the pastor and staff model evangelistic passion and lifestyles;
- Limiting the number of "competing" internal ministries and programs that are supported by the church, thereby emphasizing the significance and centrality of evangelism;
- Holding lay leaders accountable for involvement in evangelistic opportunities;
- Using personal testimonies from the newly converted to encourage and to inspire the congregation to evangelize;
- Implementing personal and practical steps toward evangelism, such as having people develop a list of individuals for whose salvation they will pray and will work toward, or challenge small-group leaders to expand their groups by inviting nonbelievers.

Most of the evangelistic churches use a number of such efforts simultaneously.

*3. The church uses events to reach people.* Most (although not all) of these Bodies utilize events designed to attract the nonbeliever. Pastors admit that putting together these events is usually hard work and represents a risk.

When seeking to facilitate decisions to follow Christ, nothing is a sure bet. Even events that work one year may be a flop the next. We found, however, that most of these leaders were willing to take reasonable risks because of their passion to penetrate circles of people that they had thus far been unable to influence.

We also found that the typical cutting-edge evangelistic church uses several events each year and changes the events from year to year, perhaps retaining one or two of the more successful events and replacing the marginal efforts with new approaches. They use a variety of events for various kinds of outcomes (i.e., preevangelism, soft evangelism, heavy evangelism), and they target events to reach specified people groups (e.g., a variety of events geared to reach families, professionals, women and ethnic groups).

The range of events is virtually unlimited. Here is a sampling of some of the events used recently by the evangelistic churches we interviewed:

- Christmas musical;
- Easter musical;
- Picnic and athletic event;
- Concert;
- Thanksgiving meal for the needy;
- Seminars, community forums;
- Youth rallies or sports parties;
- Showing an evangelistic movie;
- Businesspeople's luncheons;
- Days designated for bringing friends;
- Community fair or carnival;
- Evangelistic crusade;
- Sports clinics;
- Mother's Day or Father's Day banquet;
- Community service project;
- Neighborhood or block parties;
- Halloween alternative event;
- Planting new churches;
- Telephone hot line for counseling;
- Live nativity scene for Christmas season;
- Communitywide marathon;
- Valentine's Day banquet;
- Art fair;
- Ethnic/cultural celebration;
- Passover celebration;
- Wild-game banquet.

Such events are in addition to ongoing ministries at churches whose primary thrust is evangelistic.

Among the outreach activities that have sharing the gospel as their main objective are affinity group ministries (prisoners, convalescents, unwed mothers, homeless children, non-English speaking persons, mothers of preschoolers); seasonal programs (sports leagues, vacation Bible school); regularly offered classes (Sunday School, introductory Christianity, 12-step groups); evangelistic small groups; and other miscellaneous kinds of efforts (community development, employment training, bus ministry, tract distribution, street evangelism, radio and TV broadcasting).

*4. To foster effective evangelism, these churches study what other churches are doing and adopt and adapt liberally.* One of my personal misconceptions about cutting-edge evangelistic churches was that they would be original and innovative. Having examined the work of the leading churches, though, I certainly misjudged what makes a church a leader in evangelism. Leadership in evangelism has more to do with diligence and focus than with novelty and experimentation.

Some of the leading evangelistic churches are incredibly bold in what they dream up and try. Most of these ministries, however, develop their unusual approaches by simply staying in touch with what is happening in the evangelistic as well as the consumer marketplace, and then taking time to reflect on how to bridge those two worlds for evangelistic effect.

One pastor noted that most churches fail to innovate or to exhibit any uniqueness in what they do because they do not make time for "creative meditation" about reaching the unreached. His church stages more than a dozen evangelistic events each year, rarely repeating the same event two years in a row. The church has a reputation for developing appealing, interesting and effective events. This capacity is attributable to the fact that those people focusing on evangelism intentionally carve hours out of their busy schedules to simply dream about how to reach the non-Christian community.

One of the hallmarks of leading-edge evangelistic churches is that when they see a great idea that can be translated into their own context for outreach, they embrace that idea without hesitation.

"Look, all of these creative impulses are implanted by the Holy Spirit anyway," says a pastor who leads a church that sees several hundred people make decisions annually. "We're not the creative genius behind any of it, God is. Even if we were the source of that genius, why wouldn't I want other churches to adopt the best of what we've tried? Why wouldn't I want other brothers and sisters to discover what we've learned? I'm not in competition with other churches. I'm supposed to be supporting them, just as I hope they're supporting what we're doing here."

The evangelism director at another church acknowledged that they have brainstorming sessions and generate many novel strategies for reaching their area for Christ but admitted "we do nothing that is innovative; we've just borrowed from others."

The pastor of a Methodist church was a bit more direct in his self-assessment: "I'm not really an innovator. I'm more or less a thief."

The significance of being aware and willing to adapt methods that originate elsewhere was amplified by an Asian-American pastor who spent his first few years in this country attending seminars and visiting churches to learn the culture and how to minister effectively. His conclusion was: "I found that most of the (effective) churches use the same methods."

Creativity in evangelism, then, means knowing how to discover great ideas that can be successfully transferred to a new context and being able to improve upon those ideas and experiences.

5. *Evangelistic churches rely upon the people to do evangelism, but they also allocate an above-average amount of money for evangelistic activity.* The typical Protestant church in America spends less than 2 percent of its annual revenues on community evangelism. Among the leading evangelistic churches, however, we found that it was more common to spend 10 percent to 20 percent of the annual budget for that purpose.

The range was considerable, though. Some of these congregations only devoted 1 percent or 2 percent to local outreach. Others, however, spent as much as 50 percent on evangelism.[5] In general, the churches that are most serious about evangelism seem to put their money where their mission is.

Although experience clearly proves that the effect of a ministry is not guaranteed by investing large sums of money, the research also confirms that when money is invested intelligently, it can result in more effective evangelism than would have been possible without such financial support.

Certainly, we have seen many churches that allocate significant sums of money to evangelism and have little to show for their investments. Designating money for outreach is not, by itself, the key. However, for a ministry that has creative thinkers, passionate evangelists, strong leaders and wise strategists, providing a significant budget for evangelism can multiply the other gifts and abilities residing within the church many times over.

Even the ways the money is used for evangelism seems to differ somewhat between the evangelistically influential churches and churches that have a less discernible influence. The leaders of evangelistic churches allocate a greater portion of their funding for reaching youth.

Strategically, this makes sense. Have you ever wondered why most decisions for Christ are made by people who are under the age of 18, yet most of the money spent by churches on evangelism is aimed at changing the hearts of adults? It makes little sense.

Many of the evangelistically driven churches recognize this disparity and deploy their money where they are most likely to receive the greatest return. Although they do not avoid the adult market, they simply strike a more reasonable balance between reaching the young and old.

Ample financing of the evangelistic activity is an important precedent to releasing and maximizing the church's greatest gift to society. Money alone cannot force life transformation, but money available to smart, driven evangelizers can expand the possibilities almost beyond recognition.

*6. These churches are unique in their evangelistic structures, systems and strategies, and they do not seek to copy any other church.* I was intrigued that the pastors and evangelism directors of these congregations were generally unaware of other churches that were involved in unique, impressive, cutting-edge evangelism.

More importantly, though, was the reality that they did not bow to external pressures to conform to the prevailing manner of activity. Many of the churches we evaluated were denominational, but they generally felt the freedom to pursue courses of action that differed from those promoted by the denomination.

■ ■

## EVANGELISTIC LEADERS ATTRIBUTE THE POWER OF THEIR OUTREACH EFFORTS TO THE CONTINUITY AND INTENSITY OF THEIR PRAYER COMMITMENT.

■ ■ ■

In the course of our research, we sensed that evangelistic church members are independent thinkers, risk-takers, aggressive and restless. Even when they encountered a program, an event and an approach in another church they liked, they generally modified it substantially before implementing it. This radical independence does not always endear them to other churches, but their concern is not to curry popularity inside the church world but to have influence in the world outside of the church.

## A FEW SURPRISES

I've been studying churches for the past decade. I don't know it all, by any stretch of the imagination, but I have developed a fairly good sense of how churches work and what makes some grow and others shrink, what makes some healthy and others dysfunctional.

One of the enjoyable aspects of conducting research is that you always uncover a few unexpected outcomes. Our research among leading evangelistic churches was no exception. Five findings surprised me. Maybe they won't surprise you, but I believe these conditions are worth noting.

### CONDITIONS WORTH NOTING
*The evangelistic efforts of these churches were not constantly supported by prayer.* I do not know any Christian who would refute the power of prayer or the

biblical mandate we have to communicate with God continually through a serious life of prayer. Virtually every Christian leader I know espouses the importance of beseeching God, through sincere and persistent prayer, to bless our lives and our efforts to serve Him.

Therefore, I was amazed to learn that many of the most evangelistically powerful churches have only a modest practical commitment to prayer. I say "practical" because each of these churches acknowledges the importance of prayer, and each one has some form of prayer ministry in place.

Among the evangelistic leaders, we found a few who live a life of prayer. They attribute the power of their outreach efforts to the continuity and intensity of their prayer commitment (e.g., 24-hour-a-day prayer by the church; praying before, during and after every service by a prayer team; preceding any event of major decision relating to evangelism with prolonged prayer and so on).

Most of the leading churches, however, had a more general-focused, universal prayer ministry in place. Amazingly, they did not have a prayer component that focused specifically upon their evangelistic efforts and objectives. (Can you imagine what might happen if they increased their involvement in prayer?)

*Few of the senior pastors at the leading evangelistic churches have the gift of evangelism.* Amazingly, we discovered that the senior pastors of these churches are passionate about turning the uncommitted into the converted, but their personal areas of giftedness generally are related to preaching, leadership or administration. They preach bold and challenging messages about evangelism, write fiery congregational letters exhorting the troops to engage in local outreach and argue forcefully for larger budgets, more events and additional training related to evangelism.

The reason evangelism was a core factor in these churches was that the senior pastor was an impassioned, indefatigable proponent of evangelism. They do not, however, push the evangelistic agenda because sharing the gospel is their personal, primary spiritual gift.

*These churches had no standard training programs, exercises or approaches in common for the purposes of equipping the laity for evangelism.* Most of these churches have some kind of formal classes, materials or other means of equipping the laity to engage in effective evangelism. Each of these churches has essentially reinvented the wheel when it comes to training people because they disliked the existing training materials and programs developed by parachurch ministries, seminaries, educational institutes and other churches.

As as result, a substantial proportion of staff time and the evangelism budget are designated to developing, testing, refining and implementing training exercises. This is probably a reflection of the congregational culture: Just as they adapt but rarely copy the evangelistic events and strategies of other ministries, so do they adapt and modify the training activities they see elsewhere.

*These churches recognize the evangelized but essentially ignore the evangelizers.* In the business sector, a well-honored principle is that effective employees need reinforcement and appreciation to retain their sense of commitment to the company, pursuit of growth and excellence and sense of personal value. Without displays of gratitude from the employer, employees are more likely to experience burnout, to leave the company or to experience a waning interest in their area of influence. The secular businesses we work with typically have incentive, reward, recognition and appreciation programs designed to bolster the confidence and sense of worth of the person who does good work. These are the people you do not want to lose for lack of acknowledgement.

The church world has yet to learn the importance of recognition. Although our research among churches in general has confirmed that few bodies have methods of thanking or calling attention to the stellar ministers of the faith, I assumed that the leading churches would be different. After all, in a society that takes great joy in ridiculing "religious zealots" and those who are willing to proclaim the virtues of biblical morality, certainly the most evangelistically minded congregations would have discovered the importance of encouraging their troops.

I found, instead, churches that paraded the new converts before the congregation to encourage the entire Body with the harvest the Lord had brought forth without mentioning that the converts' decision to embrace Christ had been facilitated through the diligent and obedient efforts of a particular person or group of people. The attention of the church Body was trained exclusively upon the evangelized, ignoring the role and model of the evangelizers.

I found that many church leaders actually resist giving plaudits to those who operate in the trenches of spiritual warfare, intentionally choosing not to acknowledge their efforts or to publicly applaud their victories. Most frequently, the argument is that any public demonstration of appreciation for the evangelizers would cross the line of appropriate recognition.

"The last thing we want to do is have people involved in evangelism because they get kudos from the pastor or because they might be able to stand before the congregation and bask in the spotlight," the argument goes. "If they are motivated by the proper reasons, their reward is from the knowledge that God used them as an instrument of grace and reconciliation."

*Most of the cutting-edge evangelistic churches have major problems with low retention of converts.* This was the most disturbing revelation of all. The conclusion I have come to is that churches are so focused on obtaining decisions that they ignore conversions. In other words, the American Church may be the living example of Jesus' concern expressed in Matthew 13:5,6: the seed sprung up in rocky places and was scorched by the sun, lacking depth of roots. It is one thing for a person to assent to follow Christ. It is quite another to then pick up his cross and bear it after making the decision.

The "back door" problem was immediately apparent upon evaluating the statistical condition of many evangelical churches. Any congregation that baptizes 500 people a year but only grows by a couple of hundred annually has a retention problem. Churches that allegedly lead 50 to 100 people to Christ each year yet remain in the 200 to 300 range in weekend attendance are struggling with the translation of decisions to conversions. A Body that rejoices about seeing 600 "documented decisions" in a 12-month period but has a head count of 3,000 people after 20 years may be effective at generating interest in Christ but perhaps is not as effective in developing fully devoted followers of Christ.

## PROBLEMS OF RETENTION

I believe we can identify three major difficulties related to the retention of new believers. The first is that most evangelistic churches have *poor tracking systems*. When it comes time to make a decision to follow Christ, many churches simply ask people to raise their hands, look up, stand up or do some other simple action during a service to indicate their decision to follow Christ. At preevangelistic or evangelistic events, no attempt may be made to identify these people.

My analysis is not to criticize churches that utilize such approaches. My objective is simply to point out that one very significant consequence is that the church cannot conduct any kind of personalized follow-up with the new believer. This is unfortunate because we also know that a person is most spiritually vulnerable immediately after choosing to turn his or her life over to Christ. Satan will do everything possible to steal the power and lasting influence of that decision.

Unless the church is ready to capitalize upon the person's determination to make Christ the Lord of his or her life, the odds are imposingly large that the person will actually move backward spiritually. Often we have seen people who are not immediately encouraged and discipled write off the experience as either emotionalism or a decision that is now behind them (i.e., they have their "fire insurance": They are protected against an eternity spent in hell and can now get on with the rest of their lives).

A second weakness relates to *inadequate discipleship* efforts. Evangelistic churches tend to major on outreach rather than inreach. Ideally, however, the Body of believers needs a balance of the two—a heart for ministry to outsiders strengthened by a dogged pursuit of personal spiritual growth, facilitated by the array of growth opportunities offered by the church. Most of the leading evangelistic churches understand the importance of follow-up, but it was not uncommon for us to hear: "We're working on that."

Most of these churches are more concerned about getting out the gospel than following up on new believers. The usual strategy is to be sensitive to the new believer and to leave the responsibility of seeking a path to spiritual development to that person.

The evidence suggests that merely availing people of classes and events that might strengthen or deepen their faith is not enough. The church must be more aggressive in assisting each person in his or her growth in the faith.

The third weakness is more strategic. The evangelistic churches constantly promote the importance of building relationships with nonbelievers so that reasonable opportunities to share the gospel will be available with these people. There is, however, a noticeable *lack of emphasis upon the mature believer taking responsibility for discipling the new believer.* Incredibly, it is assumed that the relational trust and credibility will be transferred from the person to an institution (i.e., the church) once the decision to become a follower of Christ has been made.

This is, I believe, an assumption that must be questioned, especially in light of evidence that perhaps hundreds of thousands of people who "make a decision for Christ" are lost every year between the moment of decision and the initiation of developing personal spiritual maturity.

## UP FOR GRABS

Don't get the impression that the pool of leading evangelistic churches all march to the beat of the same drummer. Virtually no consistency among these churches was noticed in several ministry aspects.

For instance, some evangelistic churches had services designed for seekers while others chose not to dally with a seeker approach. Some relied upon cell groups either as a principle means of introducing the nonbeliever to Christ or for developing the faith of the converts. Other churches had small-group programs that were dysfunctional, at best. Altar calls are *de riguer* in many of these churches. Others, in light of their philosophy of ministry and strategic perspective on reaching the modern culture, wouldn't dream of asking a person to come forward or to make any type of overt, public commitment.

A few of the evangelistically minded churches believe that a sign of effectiveness is planting new churches rather than in expanding the mother church to the largest possible size. Others contend that an increasing membership provides a necessary or superior environment for effective evangelism, given their style of ministry.

Sensitivity to the felt needs of the audience also varied substantially.

Some churches were single-minded in their desire to peg their ministry efforts to the key felt needs and life issues of the non-Christian populace while other churches waved off such concern by saying the gospel is always relevant in its most direct form.

## RULES OF THUMB

A few general rules of thumb emerged regarding church-based evangelism. One relates to routines, traditions and the predictability of evangelistic activity in view of the church's denominational ties. Although America may be entering a postdenominational age, we noticed that a church's heritage and denominational bonds often influence how it perceives its world and how it reaches out to love that world.

Southern Baptist churches are almost instantly identifiable by their language, their ministry philosophy, their outreach methods and their expectations. Foursquare and independent Pentecostal churches have their idiosyncrasies that helped them to stand out from the crowd. Mainline churches were easily distinguished from evangelical and fundamentalist churches by their philosophy of ministry and their perceptions of evangelism.

This distinctiveness related to denominationalism raises some interesting questions that churches may wish to consider in reflecting on strategic evangelism and the potential for reaching a changing culture.

As our nation has become more and more ethnically diverse, we also discovered that churches comprised of various ethnic groups champion entirely different ways of penetrating their population groups. Styles of evangelism, methods of communicating the gospel, the kinds of events that are utilized, the role of the pastor and the integration of prayer into the mix of activity often vary according to the target population. In comparing churches that are focused on reaching any one of the four major ethnic groups—Caucasian, African-American, Hispanic or Asian—we found that each has a different set of cultural obstacles they must acknowledge, understand and overcome.

For instance, churches pursuing a Caucasian constituency are the most likely to use nontraditional, soft-sell tactics. Hispanic Protestant churches often fight against the quasi-Catholic background of immigrants and must develop services and events that are sensitive to this emotional struggle for many Latinos. Asian churches often confront difficulties in reaching Asian-Americans because of the vagaries of cultural expectations and mores such as those related to privacy, respect, heritage and self-reliance. African-American congregations must address other obstacles, often related to communication styles, economic crises, authority issues and relational challenges.

The outgrowth of these diverse hurdles to sharing the gospel is a Christian Church in this nation that is increasingly defined by variety in

philosophies of outreach, methods of evangelism and mechanisms for training evangelists and for discipling new believers.

America is a geographically defined entity that no longer has a culturally
unified population. The spiritual battle within the geographic boundaries,
therefore, must respond to this cultural diversity.

The research also highlighted three emphases that evangelistic churches
take. The most common seems to be churches whose outreach efforts
revolve around what happens in the weekend services. The second kind are
churches whose evangelistic forays relate primarily to events beyond the
weekend services. The third kind are churches that concentrate on friendship evangelism without much institutional support for individual efforts of
church participants.

## THE VALUE OF DIVERSITY

A key lesson from our study of evangelistic churches is that a church that is
serious about reaching people with the gospel must have a multitude of
alternatives or entry points accessible to nonbelievers who are exploring the
value of Christianity. Reliance upon a single means or entry point designed
to usher people into a lasting relationship with Christ is insufficient.

Further, the research points out just how important it is to have a range
of churches that address the spiritual and personal needs of people in the
community from distinctive perspectives and to recognize that no single
church or evangelistic strategy is capable of reaching every nonbeliever
within the community.

Millions of nonbelievers need to be reached with the gospel. It will take
every bit of energy, creativity, determination and prayer we can muster to
create effective mechanisms for introducing these people to the real Jesus
Christ.

## NOTES

1. Do not confuse the term "evangelistic" with the label "evangelical." They stem from the
same root word, of course, but each provides a different shading to the terrain. I am using
"evangelistic" to connote those entities (i.e., people or churches or parachurch ministries)
that prioritize the act of sharing the gospel with nonbelievers and that are actively and
consistently involved in doing so. I use the word "evangelical" to refer to a person, church
or other organization that has a particular set of religious beliefs (as defined in footnote 1,
chapter 2) and is actively involved in seeking to promote those beliefs, the core of which
is the gospel. Thus, evangelicals are evangelistic. Entities that are evangelistic are not necessarily evangelicals.

2. After reading this chapter, you may wish to have a more detailed understanding of the inner workings of the evangelistic churches we studied. For a closer examination of what makes a church evangelistic and what evangelistic churches do in their efforts to win people to Christ, see *The Anatomy of an Evangelistic Church,* a 1995 report written by George Barna and available through the Barna Research Group, Ltd., P.O. Box 4152, Glendale, CA 91222-0152.

3. In this section, I will use the male pronoun for the senior pastors. This is not out of gender bias but is because every one of the senior pastors of the leading evangelistic churches we studied happened to be male. Nationally, approximately 97 percent of the senior pastors are male. Please understand that I am not disparaging the work of women who serve as pastors nor am I suggesting that women do not pastor leading evangelistic churches. We simply did not have the privilege of finding out about their ministries from their colleagues and interviewing them about their ministries.

4. For an excellent discussion of the tragedy inherent in partitioning evangelism from other aspects of ministry, see Ronald Sider, *One-Sided Christianity?* (Grand Rapid, Mich.: Zondervan Publishing House, 1993).

5. Budget figures are difficult to assess. A number of the evangelistically inclined churches we investigated claimed that 100 percent of their budget is geared to evangelism because everything they do in ministry—worship, outreach, community service, Sunday School, small groups, baptisms, discipleship, counseling and so forth—in some way relates to evangelism. We have tried, however, to obtain a more realistic assessment of money devoted to primary evangelistic efforts by identifying specific activities as evangelistic efforts: printing tracts, putting on outreach events, paying the salary of an evangelism director and so on.

Because churches generally do not use sophisticated budgeting and financial management techniques and because they do not tend to categorize their revenues and expenditures, it is difficult to determine how money is expended beyond such broad categories as space costs, payroll and "ministry." The 10 percent to 20 percent figure is a broad range but seems to be a reliable estimate of expenditures for evangelism.

# 7

# FUTURE VICTORY: SOCRATIC EVANGELISM

Jesus once chided the skeptics for their shortsightedness. "You know how to interpret the appearance of the sky, but you cannot interpret the signs of the times" (Matt. 16:3). This lamentation was simply a variation on an ancient biblical theme.

Hundreds of years earlier, David had acknowledged the importance of comprehending the cultural context for ministry and life by selecting a small unheralded, but critically important group of personal advisers to aid him in managing the nation. In choosing the men of Issachar as his special counselors, he positioned them as people "who understood the times and knew what Israel should do" (1 Chron. 12:32).

When it comes to assessing the possibilities for modern evangelism, we must adopt the same perspective as David and Jesus did. We must know our circumstances intimately if we hope to maximize our influence for the honor and glorify of God.

The preceding chapters may serve as a launching pad for understanding the audience, the strategies and the potential for evangelism.

## NEW CULTURE, NEW METHODS

Perhaps we should examine the emerging generation of nonbelievers and evaluate who they are, their perspectives on the gospel and how we might reach them with God's truth. It is important to focus on the emerging generation because research has revealed that two age groups, in particular, embrace the gospel.

One group is young people—children, teens, and perhaps, young adults. The other is the aged, who have time to reflect on their lives and the hereafter. The impending threat of death makes the question of salvation one of paramount importance and relevance to them, and they have experienced enough in life to evaluate the most promising options.

Timing is a critical factor in developing any movement or life change. This is no less true in terms of reaching people with the message of salvation. Research indicates that the greatest promise is among the young. In the stage of life, they are most open to Christianity and are forming a values system that will shape their lifestyle and character. Still curious, hopeful and unfettered by the woes and worries of the world, young people remain open to external influence in regard to spirituality.

## SOCIAL CHANGE AND YOUTH

The evidence we have been amassing in the past decade has also clarified that the social forces of change have redefined how to best evangelize the youth population. Consider the following fundamental social changes that have taken root in America in the past quarter century:[1]

- *Most young people reject absolute truth.* At the turn of the century, the existence of inalienable moral truths was taken for granted. People of all ages accepted these truths. The major challenge was what to do about them.

  Today, however, our research reveals that more than four out of every five Americans under the age of 30 contend that there is no such thing as absolute moral truth, but that all truth is relative to the circumstances, the people involved and the perspectives they possess.

  In other words, although the Bible claims something is absolutely true, most young adults will challenge that contention, demonstrating their fierce belief that no statement is to be taken at face value. Exhorting young people to accept Christ because the Bible tells them to do so is rejected as a ludicrous reason for such a choice.

- *Young people reject the imposition of beliefs.* It is not unusual to find that young adults want to draw their own conclusions. This is every bit as true today as it was 40 or 50 years ago. Young people may wind up drawing the same conclusions as their elders, but they want the satisfaction of arriving at those decisions on their own.

  In a society that breeds mistrust, skepticism and the assumption of intentional deceit by people who are pursuing their personal agendas, it is to be expected that young people will show little willingness to accept what others are recommending to them without thoroughly testing those beliefs. This is one outgrowth of their continued challenge of authority figures and prevailing philosophies.

Calling young people to accept the claims of Christ or the teachings of Christianity on the basis of history, traditional values, the widespread acceptance of Christianity or the alleged rationality of the Christian faith will raise the ire and mistrust of millions of adolescents and teenagers.

- *Young people are world-class skeptics.* These days it is not merely fashionable to be leery, contentious or skeptical. It is considered the only reasonable, intelligent response to a corrupt and selfish world. Young adults are adamant about questioning assumptions, challenging allegations and assertions, evaluating the basis of goals and objectives and discerning the motives underlying actions and proposals. Some adults are offended by such attitudes; others recognize this as a healthy dose of skepticism that may protect these people from harm in a dog-eat-dog environment.
- *Young people think differently.* The conclusions young folks arrive at these days is not the only thing that is different. The very paths they take to arrive there are different. Educational researchers have suggested that baby boomers and the preceding generations grew up in a society that trained people to use linear logic in making decisions.

For most people over 30, the common approach to making decisions is to move from point A to point B to point C, not deviating from the straight path until the conclusion is ultimately reached. Today's adolescents, however, mature in a different learning environment, one that uses different teaching techniques and different information strategies.

Computers, video games and other media enable young people to absorb large amounts of complex information and to process that data in a nonlinear fashion. They may reach the same conclusion as people who use linear processing, but the means to the end are very different. For evangelizers to present the gospel in ways that assume all young people are linear thinkers is an outdated view.

Understanding these realities about the new generation is vitally important. Just as Jesus made distinctions in His methods of outreach among Jews, Samaritans and Romans, so should we be sensitive to distinctions among the various people groups we are able to reach.

## THE BABY BUSTER PERSPECTIVE

Toward that end, it is important to study the baby busters, those people born between 1965 and 1983. We know they have different ways of communicating, different means of building and maintaining relationships, divergent goals and dreams, a unique values system, a religious upbringing unlike that of prior generations, a novel approach to allocating their time, and distinctive views on loyalty, commitment and expectations. Trying to integrate the gospel into their worldview will be exceedingly difficult unless we can understand their life perspectives and can respond accordingly.

I am gravely concerned about the buster generation.[2] Our research indicates that if present trends hold firm, the busters will be about one-third less likely than older Americans to accept Christ as their Savior. From a purely statistical vantage point, that means in comparison to the proportion of born-again Christians who are 30 and older, the busters will produce 10 million fewer people who will name Jesus as their Savior than would be expected.

This, in turn, means that we will see the church in this nation shrinking. Fewer people are likely to see heaven upon their passing from this earth, and the prospects for an expansion of evangelistic and compassion ministries will decline.

The good news, though, is that it is not too late to retool our efforts to reach this vital group of people. Most busters are still shaping their values, their philosophy of life and their loyalties. They are actually a more spiritual generation than the boomers or builders, the two generations that preceded them.

By this I mean that busters think about spiritual matters: the existence of God, the purpose of life, the meaning of forgiveness, the existence of heaven and hell and the role of humanity in the cosmic sphere. They freely discuss such matters among themselves although they are somewhat reluctant to discuss this with their elders because they neither trust nor respect the older generations. And they want to do what is right. The challenge is for them to have a realistic and appropriate framework for analysis.

## STRATEGIC EVANGELISM

We know that more than a dozen methods or approaches can be used by Christians and ministry groups to reach the unreached busters, a group in which about one out of every four is a Christian. But we can also estimate the probable success of each of the methods based on what we know about the thinking styles, lifestyles, religious views and experiences and personal needs and interests of this generation.

Rather than simply conduct evangelistic efforts that are comfortable or traditional, we must pursue the strategies that hold the greatest promise of a good return. If we simply go with what is safe, that is, what we have always done, or with what stretches us the least, we are no different than the scorned, wicked and lazy servant in the parable of the talents (see Matt. 25:24-30). Our responsibility is not to avoid risks or to do whatever feels good to us, but to glorify God by doing whatever it takes to reach those who have not yet heard the gospel.

In the accompanying chart, I have tried to estimate, based on our research, how the typical baby buster might react to evangelistic forays. This is not foolproof, of course. The quality of the outreach effort, its timing, the prayer that has preceded the effort at sharing and many other factors must be considered.

---

### TABLE 7.1

## THE ESTIMATED POTENTIAL FOR EVANGELISTIC APPROACHES

| Approach to Busters | Potential for Generating Decisions | | |
|---|---|---|---|
| | Low | Medium | High |
| Lifestyle, friendship | | ___ | |
| Family | ___ | | |
| Confrontational | ___ | | |
| Cell group | | | ___ |
| Power evangelism | | ___ | |
| Mass media | ___ | | |
| Mass crusades | | ___ | |
| Affinity-group meetings | ___ | | |
| Social-welfare outreach | | | ___ |
| Youth rallies | | ___ | |
| Concerts | | ___ | |
| Drama | | ___ | |
| Sports participation | | ___ | |
| Church planting | | ___ | |
| Traditional church services | | ___ | |
| Contemporary seeker services | | ___ | |
| Sunday School | ___ | | |
| Church-sponsored events | ___ | | |
| Socratic evangelism | | | ___ |
| Literature | ___ | | |

Ultimately, statistics are meaningless. The decision to accept or reject Christ is between the person and God, regardless of the laws of averages. The averages, however, are based on patterns of behavior that might help us know how to be more sensitive to people's openness and needs.

The gospel must remain pure and uncompromised, no matter what mechanisms are used to present it to non-Christians. But the mechanism we choose may influence their willingness or their ability to hear and to understand the significance of the message being shared.

## FOUR EFFECTIVE METHODS TO INFLUENCE BABY BUSTERS

Four methods are likely to have the greatest influence on baby busters:

1. Cell groups, provided they are discussion-oriented, nonconfrontational and nonimpositional.
2. Social welfare-ministry opportunities that utilize a soft sell.
3. Lifestyle evangelism strategy.
4. Socratic evangelism, a dialectic method that has been in vogue in past centuries but has fallen into disfavor in this century.

In the section that follows, I will discuss the Socratic approach more thoroughly because I believe it holds the greatest promise for reaching the busters.

Methods that have a moderate opportunity to reap fruit include lifestyle or friendship evangelistic efforts, power evangelism, mass crusades and approaches that are event-driven (e.g., rallies, concerts, drama, sports).

The methods that have the most limited chance of reaching busters are often those we prefer to use because we have been using them for years or because they are the most easily employed. For example, family evangelism is showing declining returns because of the lack of intergenerational respect and trust. Confrontational evangelism is a direct turnoff to most people. Worse, this insensitive method often reduces future opportunities for sharing because of the authoritative, impositional nature of the approach. Media evangelism is so unpopular among this group that it represents a bad ministry investment.[3]

Special evangelistic meetings (e.g., luncheons, guest speakers) have shown little appeal among the busters, largely because the method is too impersonal and businesslike. Crusades, which are evangelistic meetings of another sort, may flourish because of the scale of activity and the elements that are generally included in the event itself.

Church planting is largely irrelevant to busters because they do not perceive the institutional church to be important or attractive and because churches are initiated on the basis of existing contacts and relatively few

Christians and churched people relate intimately to non-Christian busters.

Neither sermons nor Sunday School classes are as persuasive a method with busters as they are among older people because busters are not as inclined to attend or to visit churches. When they do, young adults are generally seeking a visceral rather than an intellectual experience. Literature evangelism is also largely wasted on this skeptical, nonreading generation, although it may have a much greater influence among the builder and senior generations.

Let me attempt to stave off some of the inevitable angry letters that will come as a result of suggesting that evangelistic church services and Sunday School classes do not have as great a chance of influencing busters as do other outreach activities.

The Bible tells us that God's Word does not return void (see Isa. 55:11). It also exhorts us to go forth in faith and to let God worry about the results. Failing to think beyond these tremendous challenges, however, would hinder our ability to reach a dying world for the sake of Christ. Weekend activities in the church building simply do not appeal to the buster generation.

I am not condoning this condition. I am suggesting, however, that we must acknowledge the reality and devise strategies that will reach people where they are, not where we wish they were.

Evangelistic sermons can be useful if an unevangelized audience is involved. The chances of attracting an unevangelized audience are increasingly slim unless we are speaking about the non-Christian people who regularly attend churches and for whom sermons and other in-service activities have consistently failed for a prolonged period.

When young adults are present, they are more likely to respond to the relationships they may build at the church or the discussion opportunities (yes, perhaps at Sunday School) rather than to a half-hour lecture. I am not against church services or Sunday School classes. I am simply more turned on by effectiveness than by traditional activities.

## SOCRATES TO THE RESCUE

One of the most interesting revelations from our research has been how positively baby busters respond to evangelistic efforts that use the Socratic method of training. Socrates was the Athenian philosopher who lived during the intertestamental period (469-399 B.C.). As one of the leading philosophers of his day, Socrates developed an instructional method that relies upon engaging a student in a logical discussion that leads to a sound conclusion.

The key to the Socratic method is for the teacher to have mastered the matter under consideration so that he or she may ask probing, directive questions that do not manipulate the student as much as to help clarify the truth conclusion sought by the student.

Socrates would raise an issue of importance and invite a student to expound on his position on the issue. Then Socrates would ask the student how the logical inconsistencies in his comments could reasonably be

■ ■

SOCRATES HAD A FEROCIOUS DESIRE TO DISCERN RIGHT FROM WRONG AND TO UNDERSTAND HOW TO LIVE AN ETHICAL AND MORAL LIFE. UNFORTUNATELY, HE ARRIVED AT THE WRONG CONCLUSION.

■ ■ ■

explained. From that point, Socrates would lead the student by continued questioning of the logic of the student's position, never stating that the student was wrong, but simply identifying the fallacies in the argument and asking the student to explain how those fallacies could be accurate. Invariably, the student would take a journey down the path of truth, hitting obstacles here and there, changing positions many times before arriving at a logical conclusion.

Socrates was a spiritual person. He had a ferocious desire to discern right from wrong and to understand how to live an ethical and moral life. Unfortunately, he arrived at the wrong conclusion. His philosophy states that man is the center of knowable reality and that we cannot know about the nature, genesis and purposes of unseen spiritual forces or the cosmos. Consequently, Socrates believed we should focus on those elements that we could understand and influence—humankind and how we live.

He concluded that knowledge is the highest attainment of humanity because knowledge of right and wrong will motivate a person to live in harmony with those insights.

The apostle Paul, who was well aware of the teaching of Socrates and other philosophers of that era, provided the Christian corrective to this in his teaching to the Romans (see Rom. 7:15-25). Socrates's contention that the highest attainment in life is knowledge clearly contradicts what the Bible teaches (see Deut. 6:5; Eccles. 12:13; Matt. 22:37-40). Socrates is certainly not the role model we wish to propose to modern-day seekers of truth!

## SOCRATIC METHOD USEFUL WITH BUSTERS
The training model that Socrates perfected is, however, a useful tool with

the buster generation because it is discussion oriented. Busters love to dissect reality, to argue about it, to reflect on the arguments they have heard and to draw conclusions for further debate. Busters, in general, love to talk.

Busters also appreciate instructional methods that do not require tacit acceptance and rote memorization of imposed principles and truths. They have little trust for people who claim to know the truth or how to gain it. That condition, they believe, differs from person to person and can only be identified through a personal discovery journey.

Further, the Socratic method differentiates knowledge from opinion, fact from feeling. Busters are an emotional group. Ordinarily, they follow their feelings and instincts unless a better nonthreatening strategy is employed. The Socratic method incorporates inductive and deductive reasoning, a process that seems less intellectually suffocating to the busters than other popular instructional methods.

This approach is relational in nature. It involves other people in the process and usually takes several meetings before a conclusion is reached on a weighty matter. This enables closeness among the participants and initiates bonds of friendship through the discussion process. As a relational generation, this is viewed positively by young people.

Finally, this strategy is invaluable because it permits nonbelievers to truly own their faith when they decide to become Christians. They are not making a spur-of-the moment emotional decision, nor are they reacting to input during a moment of weakness. When they say they have decided to follow Jesus, they are well down the road to understanding the meaning of the faith they are accepting. Discipleship, then, is easier with them because their evangelistic encounter was their initial experience of discipleship. All they have to do is to maintain the process during the deliberations about their spiritual moorings and the role of Jesus Christ in their lives.

For the evangelizer, then, this method incorporates aspects of friendship evangelism, cell-group outreach as well as something akin to an interactive sermon. It requires a new understanding of the role of the evangelizer and the process through which the gospel ultimately takes root in the mind and heart of the nonbeliever.

## JESUS DID IT
Perhaps you are concerned about the biblicism of this approach. It is sometimes difficult to see the Socratic process at work because the Bible was not written as a verbatim record of dialogue between evangelizers and the nonbelievers of the day. It was, after all, developed in the context of rabbinic teaching, which is didactic more than dialectic. Most of the New Testament, for instance, is made up of letters from Paul to various bodies of believers. Even the synoptic Gospels are meant to be a historical record of the teach-

ings of Jesus rather than manuscripts of His conversations and encounters with His followers and doubters.

But if your concern is the scriptural support for a Socratic approach, relax. This strategy contains three primary bases of support. The first is Paul's teaching, embedded within the heart of several of his letters, that encourages believers to use every means at their disposal to effectively, and without compromising the integrity of the message, present the gospel to nonbelievers (see Rom. 11:13,14; 1 Cor. 9:19-23; also, though not from Paul, Heb. 2:3,4).

The second base of support comes from the actions of Paul and other believers who engaged in Socratic interaction with nonbelievers (see Acts 17:16-32; Acts 19:1-5) and his general exhortations (see Rom. 3:1-5; Rom. 9:19-24).

Finally, Jesus also used Socratic evangelism. For instance, when Jesus engaged the Samaritan woman at the well in conversation, His approach was to ask her probing questions about her life that eventually led her to the conclusion that Jesus was Lord (see John 4). A lawyer who wanted to justify himself engaged Jesus in conversation and Christ led the man to understand the true meaning of life through a series of pointed questions and focused commentary (see Luke 10:25-37). When some of His critics tried to trap Him for His discourse on His deity, Jesus dealt with their self-righteousness through a Socratic encounter (see John 10:31-39).

Although the Bible does not contain much dialogue to evaluate, chances are good that other instances of Socratic evangelism were used during Jesus' ministry and during the early years of the church.

### ROLL UP YOUR SLEEVES

Our refusal to use the Socratic method among young people and adults when it is appropriate would be a tragedy. But to plunge into this method without thinking it through also would be unfortunate and foolish. To aid you in your deliberations about how to fruitfully engage in Socratic evangelism, here are a few guidelines.

*Get your act together.* Before you enter into a dialogue with nonbelievers about what they believe and how their beliefs may be illogical, it is imperative that you know what you believe and why. This may be more difficult than you suspect.

Our research reveals that most Americans cannot explain why they are Christians or the core truths of Christianity, why they believe the Bible is true or why other religions are false. The data also show that Americans struggle to explain their consumer patterns, their relational habits, their lifestyle preferences, their sexual expectations and their financial management practices. In short, we act reflexively rather than strategically.

The failure to know why you believe in Christianity, the specifics of your theology and the relationship between your spiritual convictions and major life issues will undermine your ability to become an effective Socratic evangelist. In reality, each of us should work through those issues, if we have not done so already, as a means of understanding and strengthening our own faith.

In the context of dialogical evangelism, the ability to carry on an intelligent, thoughtful conversation about your faith is imperative. When a nonbeliever asks a question and wants a sincere description of the Christian perspective, hiding behind simplistic explanations such as "because the Bible says so" won't get you very far. The Bible may make the claim that you have asserted, but to a nonbeliever who is not ready to buy into the Bible and who wishes to know how to relate biblical principles to everyday life, having a more substantive discourse on the core of your faith is critical.

*Be ready.* Effective Socratic evangelizers have thought through the positions and questions of nonbelievers and are ready to deal with the weighty issues likely to be raised. You cannot anticipate every question. By trying to be ready for some of the directions a conversation might take, however, you will facilitate your task of helping nonbelievers articulate their views and address the most pertinent questions.

*Practice.* Most of us are unaccustomed to holding prolonged conversations about our faith in which we are taking neither an offensive nor a defensive posture but are merely asking pointed questions that enable someone else to think more clearly about his or her faith journey and theological convictions.

Sometimes when we get into a discussion about our faith with a nonbeliever, we wind up feeling cornered or defensive as we attempt to explain away some petty concerns raised about Christianity. At other times, we may sense an evangelistic opportunity and take the offensive that sadly, may offend the nonbeliever. It may prove advantageous to prepare for a Socratic encounter with a non-Christian by having a similar discussion with a believer and getting the feel for how this approach works.

It is more natural and comfortable for some people than others, but for most people it takes some getting used to because the objective is not to argue and to win but to listen and to pose directive questions. Practice can only enhance your ability to think like an educator rather than like a debater.

*Redefine your notion of evangelism.* For many evangelizers, the act of sharing the faith with a nonbeliever is just that—an act that occurs in one place, at one time and then is completed.

In the Socratic process, you are engaging in a multipart, long-term conversation in which both parties are stretched spiritually. This is not "hit and run" evangelism based on your agenda. This is an interactive spiritual exploration with a defined goal. Evangelism, from this approach, takes longer than the typical confrontational strategy. But the results are longer lasting, too.

*Make a friend.* Socratic evangelism is geared to a fairly intense and intimate personal relationship. It would be difficult to process the kind of information required in the dialogical journey without feeling ever closer to your counterpart in that journey.

Although Socrates approached his encounters as a teacher instructing a student, the evangelizer has a different perspective—as a facilitator assisting

■ ■

## HEARING FOR THE UMPTEENTH TIME THAT "GOD LOVES YOU AND HAS A WONDERFUL PLAN FOR YOUR LIFE" MAY HAVE LOST ITS ABILITY TO CUT THROUGH THE INFORMATION CLUTTER.

■ ■ ■

a fellow explorer. Every person you engage in a Socratic dialogue may not become a close friend. It would be useful, however, if the evangelist were open to such a possibility.

Often, evangelizers become emotionally intense when sharing their faith. That is to be expected. After all, they are describing the most important person and process in their lives. Although this emotional edge may be easily understood and defended, it also is likely to hinder the Socratic encounter.

It is not that we want the nonbeliever to make a strictly intellectual decision to follow Christ, devoid of any emotional content. That is neither feasible nor desirable. Instead, we simply want to be sure that our emotions do not get in the way of a substantive, articulate, logical path to seeing the truth and integrity of Christianity.

Ultimately, the nonbeliever must feel emotionally comfortable with, and excited about, Christianity for the faith to make a real difference in his or her life. It is our task, though, as the evangelizers, to keep our emotions in check so that the focus of the dialogue is not on personal opinions and feelings but upon a reasoned understanding of Christianity.

*Be real.* One of the most disheartening findings regarding evangelism is that a large proportion of evangelizers share their faith with non-Christians the same way, every time, regardless of who the nonbeliever is or what the circumstances may be.

We have found, in contrast, that the people who are most effective at sharing their faith are those who are most lifelike—that is, the people who do not fall back on formulas, stock answers and tired phrases, but who are genuinely engaged in a creative conversation with the seeker.

Part of the reason fresh communication is effective is because of a factor noted earlier in this book: Nonbelievers already have been exposed to most of the canned, standardized approaches to telling the gospel. Hearing for the umpteenth time that "God loves you and has a wonderful plan for your life" may have lost its ability to cut through the information clutter. The approach is neither inaccurate nor spiritually inappropriate. It just may not be effective after a while. Variation and innovation in conveying a message is useful.

The data also show that the ability to relate information to personal experience and to be vulnerable in the process (i.e., not knowing all the answers, but being willing to explore puzzling questions and discover the answer) is also beneficial. In the end, nonbelievers want to feel as though they are conversing with a fellow sojourner, not a know-it-all or a master salesman.

## STARTING THE CONVERSATION

The Socratic approach is most effective when it is used as a natural part of a conversation or relationship. Attempts to force a dialogue backfire. People are insulted by a contrived attempt to push them into a line of thought.

One of the skills of the effective Socratic evangelist is to know when is the right time to pursue a conversation about deeper truths and when is the right time to simply work on building a relationship that eventually will give way to a spiritual-oriented discussion.

Initiating the conversation is generally most effective when a grand statement is made by the nonbeliever, not as a challenge, but as a statement of fact. The Christian may then politely and nonthreateningly—almost out of amazement—ask about the assumption on which the statement is built.

The second key, at this point, is to be sensitive to whether the seeker is presently comfortable to pursue any deeper line of reasoning, does time permit such a discussion, is the environment conducive to such interaction, is the bond between the two people sufficient to allow for continued probing and challenging.

If the conversation continues amicably—a Socratic encounter for evangelistic purposes must always be friendly, never mean-spirited or hostile. A third key is to know when to conclude the conversation. The chances of starting and completing the spiritual journey of discovery in one sitting are slim. Usually, the process consumes several unscheduled, informal but purposeful sessions.

The Christian is usually the one who must subtly and gently (but not apologetically) broach the subject matter for the continued discussion. Knowing when to end and when to reinitiate a conversation is crucial. We must read the context and read the state of our colleague to know when to continue the process.

Often, as the conversation nears an end and the nonbeliever is coming to a reasonable conclusion, the believer may have an opportunity to interject some element of his or her own spiritual journey and personal conclusions. The purpose of this is to shift the nature of the conversation from one of constant challenging through questioning to one of mutual understanding.

"I've been this route myself and had to address these same questions, and here's where I've landed on the matter," the questioner might say. "It's the only thing that makes sense for me."

This kind of factual testimony in this context may further encourage the nonbeliever to take a step of faith and name Christ as personal Lord and Savior. Rushing to insert a testimony too quickly in the conversation, though, can undermine the trust and the process of reflective consideration that have been built. Again, sensitivity is crucial.

## A SOCRATIC CONVERSATION

There is no standard structure or script to follow in an evangelistic encounter using Socratic methods. But consider how such a dialogue might transpire in the course of a natural conversation.

"I can't believe that these self-righteous, old-fashioned, power-hungry politicians are going to try to institute a constitutional amendment to allow prayer in public schools," Bill, a nonbeliever says. "Prayer is a private matter. They should just leave the law as it stands now rather than forcing people to pray."

"That's an interesting position, Bill," Tom, a believer says while ignoring the erroneous reference to the alleged amendment "forcing people to pray." Tom recognizes that reference does not address the real issue. "So I guess you believe that prayer is not to be said in public?"

"That's right. People should not have to engage in any religious behavior that is against their beliefs, their principles, their will, you name it. Religion is such a private matter, we shouldn't have to do anything if we don't feel like it."

"Bill, you pay taxes, don't you?"

"Yeah."

"When you send in your tax payment in April, or look at all of the tax dollars withheld from your paycheck each month, do you pay taxes because you feel like it?"

"What are you, nuts? It *feels* like extortion. Who enjoys paying taxes?"

"Well, I sure don't, and I figured you probably don't either. In fact, I recently read that the typical American now works until June each year just to pay off his taxes. Then the income the rest of the year—barely more than half of the year—is income he can use to live on. For all the talk in Washington about tax relief, it sure doesn't seem to have filtered down to the average guy. But when I think about taxes, it strikes me as a behavior we engage in even though we don't particularly enjoy it, or even want to. Yet we do it. Why should we pay taxes?"

"Tom, can you imagine the problems we'd have if people didn't pay their taxes? The deficit is already out of control. Tax fraud already costs the government billions in lost revenues, which then hinders the government's ability to carry out its business and to institute its programs and services. I guess I pay my taxes out of habit, but it's a habit based on the assumption that I have an obligation to other people and that ultimately I receive benefits from paying my fair share."

"I think I pretty much follow the tax laws for the same reasons as you. But Bill, we're both basing our behavior on two critical points: obligation and benefit. Thinking about the prayer issue, what if Congress did pass a constitutional amendment allowing the public expression of one's beliefs in public schools. Is there any benefit to praying? Does a person have a personal obligation to pray to his or her God?"

"Hmm. I guess it depends on the person and what they think about prayer."

"Yeah, it's kinda interesting, isn't it? And here's another question that pushes the issue even further. Why do people pray? What is the purpose of prayer? I believe people's answers to these questions often help them determine what kind of 'rights' and laws should be established regarding this whole controversial issue. Do you ever pray?"

"Well, sure, sometimes. I mean, I don't pray all the time, but there are some times, you know, like when you're in a real crisis situation or something, when you pray."

"Yeah, I've been there. That car accident I had three years ago, when my convertible was totaled. Man, I thought I'd been hit by a tank. When I came to, I didn't have my bearings, but I was praying all the way to the hospital. Why do you think we pray when we get in those kind of serious situations?"

"I don't know. Maybe because things seem so far out of our control."

"But why pray? Why not just cry or give up or get angry or do anything else than pray? Think about the times you've prayed. Why bother? What's the use? Why do we do it?"

"For me, I guess it's because I feel powerless. I can't make things go the way I want. I'm scared and I want to restore some degree of control and regularity to my circumstances. I want things to be normal again."

"But doesn't that mean some power exists that is greater than us that we trust or rely upon? Just who or what are you praying to? It seems to me that we pray because we have certain assumptions about what prayers can do, assumptions about what prayer means and how it affects our lives. I do the same thing as you. When I'm in a tight spot, once I get some perspective on the situation, once I realize I can't do much about it on my own but I sure don't want the situation to remain static, then I start to pray. Have you ever thought much about it? It's really interesting to me. I find that most people do the same thing you and I do. And I think a key part of all of this is who we pray to. Who do you pray to when you're in those tight spots?"

"God, of course."

"Yeah, but you know, everybody says that. What does that really mean? What or who is God? When you're struggling and you start praying to God, there have to be some assumptions you've got about this God that we pray to. I know I certainly have those assumptions. When you pray to God, what does that mean? Who is God for you? And why would you pray to God instead of to the doctors that are bandaging you or to the cop who has pulled you over to the side or to the professor who holds the outcome of your academic career in his hands?"

"Tom, I haven't thought much about it. It's always just seemed kinda automatic. You know, we're brought up to pray to God. I've never really thought much about it, other than to know that God isn't very real in my life. I don't even know if there is one."

"But then why would you pray to God? Either you're foolishly praying to something that doesn't exist or you're intelligently praying to a power source that you don't yet understand. Or maybe there's another reason or motivation. What do you think?"

This conversation, of course, is far from complete, but I believe you have a clue of how a Socratic encounter might transpire. Various levels of intellectualism can be woven into the conversation. This example used a rather light intellectual approach because the relationship was based on fairly unsophisticated discussions. But this short example serves to drive home a few other points that are germane to effective Socratic evangelism.

## THINGS TO REMEMBER

*Reinforce reasonable conclusions.* It is valuable to provide subtle reinforcement to the appropriate conclusions drawn by our counterparts in this process. We do not want to overtly applaud their solid reasoning because we do not want to caricature the intellectual process by which they are arriving at these answers. On the other hand, it is useful to underscore the appropriate conclusions they reach, encouraging them to continue on the path of discovery without transcending the line of manipulation.

*Ask questions, but don't set yourself up to answer them.* The natural tendency in American education is to lecture, to tell others the answers then to get them to parrot those answers in controlled scenarios. Socratic training requires the teacher to pose questions that allow the student to develop a response and to test that response logically with the assistance of additional questions from the facilitator.

Asking questions in a manner that leads the facilitator to field the questions of the seeker is counterproductive, minimizing the intellectual growth of the seeker and the seeker's ownership of his or her conclusions.

*Have a sense of purpose and direction.* Stay focused on your objective. In such conversations, it is very easy to get sidetracked. Sometimes that will happen. It's better to let that discussion die than to try to artificially restore life to it. The most effective means of preventing such a diverted interaction is to process all information through a mental filter, one that maintains a clear and constant focus on the objective.

*Move at a comfortable pace.* Sometimes we want to get to the final point, the "Jesus is Lord and you must accept Him and thereby have eternal life, peace with God, meaning in life" and so forth. This zeal for loving nonbelievers into God's everlasting presence is laudable, but we have to be careful that our love for them does not frighten them away from God. Move at a pace that seems reasonable given your relationship with the person, the cues they are sending regarding the discussion and the prompting of God's Holy Spirit.

*Use biblical principles without citing chapter and verse.* If you're like most of us, the temptation will be to reply to some of the more ludicrous comments of the nonbeliever by using statements such as: "But in Romans 1:21 God deals with that very issue."

To most nonbelievers, the Bible is not a definitive reason for taking a stand on an issue. It may be interesting, but it may also prove counterproductive to the overall thrust of the conversation. The same effect can be had, in most cases, by using the wisdom and truth contained in the Bible as the element that steers the conversation toward a God-pleasing conclusion. Once the individual is open to hearing the perspectives of God, then citing biblical principles is necessary and desirable.

*Sometimes it takes multiple conversations on multiple issues.* A discussion about prayer, for instance, might lead more easily into beliefs about God and eternity than would a discussion about the ethical basis of our social welfare program or the importance of marriage.

In such instances, it makes sense to pursue these issues to their logical conclusion, rather than to await another opportunity at another point in time to pursue yet another issue to a conclusion that may move the person closer to recognizing his or her need to accept the majesty of God.

## PROPER TIMING

Believers who wish to engage in Socratic evangelism must be prepared at all times to engage in such conversations, much as they must be ready at any moment to explain to anyone what they believe about their faith and why they embrace that faith system (see 2 Tim. 4:2; 1 Pet. 3:15). An effective evangelizer is one who has made outreach a priority and is constantly alert to opportunities to facilitate a nonbeliever's search for truth and meaning in life.

A discussion about absolutely any issue or situation in life could potentially lead to a conversation about God and eternal matters. Questions that might spark such a dialogue involve issues that raise the meaning and purpose of life (e.g., suicide, euthanasia, feelings of inadequacy or aimlessness), situations that question the existence of God or any supreme power, the matter of morality and values (e.g., ethics violations in government, white-collar crime, public discussion about family values or traditional values). Other issues might be situations that require forgiveness (e.g., adultery, lying, unjustifiable outbursts of anger or hostility, international wars), the historicity of God or Jesus Christ (e.g., the Creation, Christmas, Easter), the meaning of love (e.g., marriage or parenting difficulties).

At the heart of every single public or private issue we struggle with is our worldview. At the heart of our worldview is our faith system and spiritual beliefs. In some manner, then, every significant decision we make and every important opinion we hold is rooted in our theological perspectives, whether or not we have clearly and intentionally articulated those perspectives.

But we are most effective when we do not force the issue. When the timing is right, God will provide the openings. We simply have to be prepared to take advantage of the opportunities He provides. Socratic evangelism may be one means of maximizing some of those opportunities.

## NOTES

1. For a deeper analysis of the young generation, a growing body of research data and analysis is available. You might consider the following: George Barna, *Generation Next* (Ventura, Calif.: Regal Books, 1995); George Barna, *Baby Busters* (Chicago: Northfield Publishing, 1994); Josh McDowell and Bob Hostetler, *Right Vs. Wrong* (Dallas: Word Inc., 1994).
2. For the sake of clarity, America currently has five generations. The labels I use for them are the *seniors*, people born in 1926 or before, roughly 40 million strong; the *builders*, those born from 1927 to 1945, about 43 million strong; the *baby boomers*, the largest generation ever in America, 79 million people born from 1946 to 1964; the *baby busters*, the second largest generation ever, 68 million people born from 1965 to 1983; and the

*unnamed generation* that trails the busters. It is unnamed because we do not yet know enough to label them, of undetermined size because this generation will extend from 1984 through to 2002.

3. Please be aware that I am not among those who say that if we spend a million dollars on broadcasting and just one soul comes to Christ because of that investment, it was all worth it. That soul is terribly important to God, and a million dollars is a paltry sum in God's economy to lavish on reaching the person. We know, however, that for the same million-dollar investment, many, many more people than a single human being could have been reached and turned on to Christ. The issue is one of stewardship, which involves efficiency of resource allocation. If we had unlimited resources for reaching the world, this might not be an issue. We do not, however, and never will have unlimited resources. Someday, when we are asked to account for how we used the resources God entrusted to us, we will not want to hide behind the "soul at any cost" argument. After all, God created accountants.

# 8

# RESTORING EVANGELISTIC POWER IN OUR CHURCHES

During the next decade, America's population will explode by 15 million people. But even that figure masks the true growth we will experience because it only reflects our net growth, which is based on the number of births and immigrants minus the number of deaths.

The total number of new Americans that will join us during the coming decade will reach about 45 million people. That enormous group of people—more than now reside in California, Oregon and Washington—will be mostly newborns.

From an evangelistic standpoint, we will have a rapid expansion in opportunities to share the gospel because 44 million of the newcomers will be non-Christian. The exception will be the relatively few immigrant children and adults who will enter the country as Christians. The vast majority of immigrants, however, will enter as nominal Catholics who do not have a relationship with Christ.

## A MONUMENTAL CHALLENGE

Our Christian churches have a monumental challenge of reaching the current non-Christian population of 190 million people plus the anticipated horde of 45 million newcomers. That adds up to 235 million people who live on American soil—nearly a quarter of a billion souls.

To complete such a task of sharing the gospel with those people is going to consume every ounce of energy and every resource we can muster. Time is of the essence in this battle, for we do not know when a person will die, nor when the Lord will return for His people en masse. It is imperative, therefore, that we increase the intensity of our efforts to fulfill the Great Commission from Jesus to His followers.

We cannot dispute the fact that as we attempt to penetrate the spiritual darkness that engulfs America, we are engaging in a spiritual battle for the souls of humankind (see Eph. 6:10-18). Unlike modern armies that rely on government budgets, sophisticated machinery and international alliances to blast their ways to their objectives, our success is dependent upon the power of God.

As we seek to be obedient to our Commander's call to fight the forces of evil that dull the minds and bind the hearts of nonbelievers, we are reminded that one of the primary strategic warriors in this battle is the local church.

# THIRTEEN OBSTACLES TO EFFECTIVE EVANGELISM

Although we have discussed what some churches are doing to fight the good fight, this chapter will identify 13 obstacles to effective church-based evangelism that we must overcome if we wish to truly put ourselves on the line for Christ.

As you read these obstacles, consider if the weakness applies to your church. If so, for the sake of the nonbelievers in your midst and for the glory of God, please pray and think about what you and your church can do to enhance its ministry in relation to an identified weakness.

## THE ABSENCE OF PRAYER
A church that strives to evangelize its community without saturating its efforts in prayer is like a race-car driver that jumps into his car at the starting line and discovers that the tank has not been filled with gasoline. We cannot hope to influence the hardened hearts and stray souls of humankind without inviting God to empower and bless our meager efforts on His behalf.

The most compelling models of church evangelism emerge from churches that engage in consistent, abundant prayer for the outreach ministry. As you examine your church's evangelism activities, are they preceded by specific prayer for the ensuing efforts? Do the people who engage in personal interaction with non-Christians spend significant amounts of time praying for God's direction and blessing?

Is the church at large supporting the efforts of soldiers on the front lines of evangelism with intercessory prayer for evangelizers and for nonbelievers who will be exposed to the gospel as a result of the church's outreach? Are the people in positions of leadership proving their fitness for leadership by living lives filled with prayer and by encouraging others to join them in begging God for mercy, power, guidance and effectiveness?

The beauty of prayer is that God answers the prayers of those who are striving to do His will, and it costs us nothing to request His blessing. The choice not to pray makes a serious statement about our trust in God. The refusal to pray also provides a debilitating comment regarding our ignorance or arrogance when it comes to the spiritual battle we wage.

## OWNING OUTREACH

Do all of the people in your church view evangelism as a central mission of the ministry and a personal responsibility? Sadly, our research shows that in most churches, only a core of people have a passion for evangelism and the mass somehow justify their own lack of participation in outreach. We have also identified entire churches that are comfortable with the notion that they are not called to evangelism because they are not "evangelical" churches.

Every church is called to be evangelistic simply because every church is nothing more than the sum of the believers who comprise that Body. And every believer has been called to evangelize. The question to explore is whether your church has integrated evangelism as part of the culture and personality of the church. Do people "own" evangelism as the heartbeat of the ministry? Is evangelism deemed the highest priority of the church? Have the people caught a special vision for reaching nonbelievers that gives the church definition, energy and direction? If not, the organization is not truly a church but is simply a group of people intrigued by religion. The Church of Jesus Christ is one that takes His command seriously and places evangelism at the heart of all of its activities.

If your church has not made evangelism the centerpiece of its ministry, get on your knees and pray for forgiveness from God as well as for wisdom on how to reinvigorate the church so that it is evangelistic in nature. Pray for your pastor as he or she seeks to lead the church forward for God's purposes. Explore the ways your budget should reflect the evangelistic priority.

Think through means of instilling a holy passion for lost souls in the hearts of the believers who call your church their spiritual home. Ask the Holy Spirit to renew your leaders and to motivate all of the believers. Restructure your roster of ministries so that each has a responsibility to incorporate evangelistic activity. Take evangelism as seriously as God does.

## BUILDING BRIDGES

One church I worked with a few years ago had developed a desire to reach the community for Christ. The members prayed. They structured their activities to reach the nonchurched and the non-Christian. The church failed to grow primarily because the members of that congregation did not personally know any nonbelievers. They read newspaper articles, magazine stories and books about nonbelievers. They listened to sermons about nonbelievers. But they had not invited any nonbelievers into their lives. When it came time to share the good news with their friends, their friends already knew because their friends were churched Christians.

Sometimes it is difficult to befriend non-Christians. They often think, speak and act very differently than we do, often in ways that are in direct conflict with the Word of God. We are much more comfortable around those who share a common bond in Christ. Our mutual love for Christ and commitment to building His Church gives us an immediate shared perspective and a sense of kinship.

But therein lies the paradox: How can we hope to influence the non-Christian population with God's truths and principles if we do not have a pathway to their hearts? That pathway is the trail of friendships we develop with those people.

Have you ever asked the people in your church to write down the names of every non-Christian person in the local area with whom they are good friends? You might be surprised at how few names would appear on those lists. Yet, it is that group of nonbelievers we are called to reach through the credibility of an authentic, caring friendship.

It is the church-sanctioned practice of turning inward—that is, to only befriend other believers—that nullifies the evangelistic influence of thousands of churches. Lacking any discernible influx of visitors or nonbelievers, the church then takes on an inward focus in which resources are devoted solely to the needs of the saints instead of having a balance between inreach and outreach.

Challenge the people in your church to identify the names of friends who are not Christians and for whom they will consistently pray and with whom they will intentionally seek opportunities to share the love of Christ. Consider having special gatherings at which you will pray together for these people, talk about meaningful ways of reaching out to these friends and rejoice in the people God has ushered into His kingdom as a result of the efforts of believers in your midst.

Challenge your people to undertake activities for the primary purpose of meeting new people and having the opportunity to build relationships with them. Examples: joining sports teams not affiliated with a church or church league, serving as a teacher's aid in a preschool setting to get to know other parents, throwing a summer block party to meet neighbors or inviting coworkers to your house for dinner. We cannot change people if they do not know us. We must take the initiative in developing these relationships.

## SEEKING THE RIGHT OUTCOME

I am convinced that much of the difficulty of church-based evangelism is that we seek *decisions* for Christ rather than *conversions*. A decision may be as simple as repeating the "Sinner's Prayer" with no real follow-through after that act. A conversion, on the other hand, is a total life transformation in which the decision to follow Christ results in a new lifestyle, a new heart for people and for God and a determination to live for totally different ends.

Jesus understood the difference between a decision and a conversion. He spoke of the distinction in Matthew 13 in the parable of the sower. Four kinds of conclusions to evangelistic efforts unfold in this story.

The first, which is most common in America, is that the seed falls on ripe soil but is snatched away before it can penetrate. People's attention is constantly diverted from the truth of the gospel, even when they have been in the presence of its proclamation.

The second scenario occurs when the seed falls upon a rocky area that contains little soil. The seed may grow, but without any roots it will quickly be scorched by the sun and die. How many people do you know who were "led to Christ," said the requisite prayer for forgiveness and then never made any further progress in their newfound faith? It may well be because they had no roots in that faith. They were not adequately discipled in their faith.

The third kind of seed is that which falls on good soil, begins to take root but withers because the cares of the world lure the person from his or her intention to pursue a life of godliness and involvement with Christ.

The fourth soil is that which produces good fruit. It is deeply rooted, well nurtured and healthy.

We do nonbelievers a disservice if we introduce them to Christ, have the privilege of seeing them decide to follow Christ, but then leave them on their own to grow. The period immediately following the decision leaves the new believer incredibly vulnerable to the darkest tricks of the enemy.

For us to abandon the new believer at that point is akin to recruiting a new soldier into the army, then immediately throwing that person into battle without training or armor. The new soldier doesn't stand a chance. He is susceptible to all of the attacks of the enemy without any means of protection. The failure to enfold and to disciple a new believer is not only a tragic sin against the new believer, but also is an offense against the God who called us to evangelize.

How does your church handle the joint responsibilities of evangelism and discipleship? If you do not have a strong support system in place to help mature a new believer, you must seriously question the validity of being involved in evangelism.

Our research shows that many nonchurched people at one time had made a decision to follow Christ, but, lacking any postdecision encouragement and education in their newfound faith, pursued worldly paths instead. They are not likely to return to the church or to ever get close to God because they assume that they have tried Christianity and have found it lacking. Much like the person who has had an evil spirit depart only to return with seven who are more evil and wicked, leaving the person worse off than he was originally, so is the person who accepts Christ and then enters the spiritual wasteland (see Matt. 12:39-45). We hurt those people more than we help them by failing to fulfill our duty of leading them to Christ and of nurturing them in that relationship.

## THE PASTOR'S ROLE

Who is responsible for making evangelism happen at your church? In most cases, if anyone has that charge, it is the senior pastor. But we must ask "why?" No place in the Bible are we told that the responsibility for inciting the people to evangelize rests solely or even primarily on the shoulders of

■ ■

### THE PASTOR MUST PROVIDE TRUE LEADERSHIP IN ALL DIMENSIONS OF MINISTRY ACTIVITY, INCLUDING EVANGELISM.

■ ■ ■

the pastor. Scripture clearly underscores that every one of us, regardless of our spiritual gifts or our formal education, are to share the love of Christ with those with whom we have contact (see Matt. 28:18-20; 1 Pet. 3:15).

At the same time, the pastor, if he or she is to fulfill the role of the shepherd, must do more than preach. The pastor must provide true leadership in all dimensions of ministry activity. Such leadership must influence several areas: teaching, modeling, training, evaluating, encouraging, exhorting, praying and sending. Although it is unhealthful to wait for the pastor to make evangelism happen within the church, it is similarly unhealthful to minister in a church where the pastor provides no leadership in the realm of outreach.

If you participate in a congregation where the pastor has the sole or primary responsibility for motivating outreach activity, pray to God to help you understand your role in that ministry. Pray to God that He will raise up more laborers to engage in the work of harvesting the souls prepared by God (see Matt 9:37,38).

Pray that the Lord will instill wisdom and direction within the heart of your pastor so that he or she might equip, empower and release the entire congregation to evangelize. And you should personally commit to God that you will begin to participate in reaching out with the message of salvation to those who have never heard it.

If, on the other hand, your church flounders evangelistically because of a lack of strong pastoral leadership, speak with your pastor about that concern. Indicate how imperative it is that your church have strong leadership in that arena and that you and many others are anxious to follow the evangelistic vision laid out for the congregation by the pastor. Pray for that pastor. And encourage him or her to action by modeling it in your life.

## DEVELOPING STANDARDS

What are the evangelistic goals and objectives of your church for the year? How is evangelistic activity tracked? When are the results reported? Who is held accountable for those outcomes?

Tens of thousands of churches go through the motions of developing numerical goals for their evangelism efforts. The problem is that there is no accountability for reaching those goals. No one is given the responsibility for tracking progress toward those desired results. No means of consistently updating the people on moving toward those ends is in place. The goals become an end in themselves: The church set standards for evangelism, "proving" it is an evangelistically minded body, which is sufficient in itself to justify continuing the church.

This thinking is deadly. It is one thing to set goals, another to reach them. Goals that do not stimulate a church to strategic action are not goals but are simply smoke screens. But God sees through that veil. Going through the motions does not impress Him, and it certainly does not reach a lost and dying world. If you serve with a group that has the foresight and ability to develop plans and goals, then carry them out.

Perhaps you serve in a church that does not do its homework, create plans, conceive strategies and minister accordingly. This is equally sad. It is like the man who does whatever comes into his mind, never thinking through the resources needed to complete the job, never considering the best means of accomplishing the desired ends. Those churches minister inefficiently and ineffectively. They are bad stewards of all resources: people, time, energy, enthusiasm, money, buildings, relationships and God's blessings.

If this is the practice of your church, it can be turned around by the prayers of those who love the church and want it to maximize its potential. Are you one of those who will pray for this kind of turnaround in your church? Can you rise up and provide the kind of leadership it will take to please God and to reach people? Can you orchestrate a team of people who are gifted in administration to work with the most ardent evangelizers toward developing plans, creating strategies and designing mechanisms for accountability? Instituting such measures will greatly enhance the evangelistic capacity of your church.

## HARDENING OF THE ARTERIES

In many churches, evangelism is thwarted by outreach programs that outlived their usefulness long ago. Unfortunately, the church is often incapable of switching paths to operate more effectively because the programs and routines have become so entrenched that changing those patterns causes extreme discomfort or confusion. The sad reality is that many opportunities to touch people's lives with the message of salvation are squandered because the evangelistic approaches are so inflexible and the people defending those systems are so insensitive to the moving of God's Spirit.

One valuable tactic is to begin each new year with "zero-base programming." This means that you start each new year with the assumption that you are starting your ministry from scratch. You may build on the existing strengths and successes, and you may abandon the preexisting flops and failures without guilt. It takes a strong and creative leader or team of leaders to pursue such an approach, but the outcome is typically much better than approaches that assume their programs and ministries are effective and only tinker with their budgets and other resources from year to year.

Yet, another means of attacking a church that has hardening of the ministry arteries is to offer ministry contracts to members. In the few churches I know of that have used this approach, the results have risen above the norm. When a person becomes a regular participant in the church (i.e., membership in traditional churches, ministry team member in more contemporary bodies), a contract is signed in which the person commits to specific kinds of service geared to identified outcomes.

During the course of the year, the person has regular review sessions with a team leader to determine how he or she is doing in meeting those ministry goals. From a programmatic point of view, this process is beneficial because it keeps the person from hiding behind systems, structures, events and other program-driven factors. Instead, the emphasis is placed upon the person's stated goals and his or her performance in reaching those objectives.

A philosophical challenge to a church that has programmed evangelism into the ground is to ensure that every ministry group within the church has an evangelistic agenda. If your church has a separate evangelism ministry, pray about the possibility of disbanding that ministry and reallocating that task to every ministry team within the church. You may still keep a team of people whose primary mission is a particular form of evangelistic activity, but you would do well to place the privilege and responsibility of outreach on the shoulders of every ministry under the auspices of your church.

## OPEN THE DOORS WIDE

Does your church assume you will reach nonbelievers through one channel of outreach? Some congregations rely upon evangelistic preaching. Some hold their small groups responsible for all outreach to nonbelievers. Others rely upon a confrontational strike team that knocks on doors throughout the community to present the story of God's grace through Christ. All of these activities are certainly good and valuable. But none of them, alone, is sufficient to reach the local world for Christ. You must have a variety of entry points through which people may enter.

Multiple entry points are developed by being sensitive to the kinds of people you wish to reach and by creating opportunities for those people to explore the claims of Christianity. You will know that you have enough entry points when you have approaches that are poorly conceived, poorly carried out or poorly tracked. It may be time to scale back. As a general rule, however, as long as you can handle the influx of new people reached through the means you have developed, you may never have too many ports of entry.

At your church, how do people receive the gospel? Are those means followed up satisfactorily? Could you institute outreach strategies that might be effective and deserve a try?

## BAD MINISTRY

Americans expect high-quality performance in everything they encountei. Salesmen must know their products and must offer good prices and excellent service. Customer service representatives have to listen to the real complaints of their customers and offer realistic and pleasing solutions. Entertainers must provide entertainment that meets the expectations of the audience in style and substance. Government leaders must move the nation forward while taking care of the needs of competing interests. And those people who serve God must provide high-quality experiences to those who wish to be in His presence, because we are serving people through our service to God (see Col. 3:23).

Your evangelistic activity may not be as glitzy or as high-powered as others might be able to sustain, but are you truly doing everything possible to raise the standard of excellence in your own context for ministry? Would outsiders look at your efforts on behalf of Christ and understand that you are driven to do your best because of your awe for Him and your perception that anything less dishonors God? Bigger is not always better. Louder is not always heard. More bizarre does not always capture more people's attention. But being honest about who you are as a church, and squeezing every last ounce of quality out of your efforts can make a big difference in the minds of those people you wish to reach.

## PREPARING THE SAINTS FOR THE TASK

Earlier in this book, I cited our research showing that only one out of every three churches offers some kind of formal training for people who wish to engage in evangelism. This is not, by itself, problematic because many parachurch ministries are training believers in evangelistic outreach. What may be indefensible, however, is for churches to totally disregard the importance of preparing people for effective outreach.

Does your church provide on-site, hands-on training in how to effectively interact with nonbelievers? If not, does the church recommend or facilitate your involvement in specific ministries or church-based training endeavors? Offering this kind of practical encouragement and preparation is imperative. Sharing our faith with Christ does not come naturally to most people. It is a multistage process that should be carefully thought through, prayed about, implemented and followed up.

The typical church can certainly provide some degree of equipping. After all, we are speaking about basic Christian apologetics and basic means of effective interpersonal communications. Helping people to know, to understand and to use the basic principles in these areas is something that churches should be teaching their people already. If you find that your church does not prepare people for effective outreach, then make sure that it at least recommends ministries that can offer such crucial ministry lessons.

## RESPONSIBILITY WITH AUTHORITY

Our research shows an inconsistency in many churches when it comes to giving away the ministry—that is, giving the people doing the ministry work the responsibility (no problem) and the authority to carry out their plans (problem).

Many pastors, staff members and other church leaders find it difficult to totally give up control and to allow people interested in evangelism to use their gifts without strict guidelines and limiting parameters. Often, the restrictions from the people who wish to maintain authority so severely hinder evangelism that even the most talented and godly evangelizers become frustrated and see their ability to minister greatly reduced.

The real issue to address in such situations is control: Who has it and how deftly is it exercised? Naturally, a church does not want to have an evangelistic presence in the community when it has no guidelines, no standards and no accountability. But a degree of freedom must exist and a measure of control must be granted to the people who are putting themselves on the firing lines. One of the marks of effective leadership is the ability to identify qualified people, to prepare them for action and to release them to do what they do best with not just verbal blessings but with the mandate to do what is necessary to get the job done in a manner that meets the existing standards and accomplishes defined goals.

In your church, do the evangelizers have the freedom to share the gospel with the community in ways that maximize their personal strengths? Does the church approve goals for outreach, then battle the evangelizers when they have a need for resources or need permission to take risks? Consider

■ ■

# WHEN CHURCHES WORK TOGETHER, THEY ARE ABLE TO ACCOMPLISH MUCH MORE THAN WHEN THEY WORK INDEPENDENTLY.

■ ■ ■

how your church might most effectively prepare people to get the gospel into the world and then support those people with whatever it takes to be successful.

## INTERCHURCH UNITY

I have been surprised at how often non-Christians tell us that churches apparently cannot agree on core spiritual issues. This sends the message that Christianity has no absolutes and is not so much about unity and cooperation as it is about competition and supremacy.

Indeed, it seems hypocritical to proclaim that all Christians are one in Christ, a true family of believers united behind Jesus, then watch as denominations, individual churches and Christians from different ends of the theological spectrum rip each other to shreds in the name of love, compassion and unity.

No church in the community is meant to be the recipient of every soul. God has allowed a variety of churches to spring up because each has the ability to minister to a certain segment of people in a way that is more effective than other churches could at a certain point in the person's life cycle and spiritual maturity. It also is demonstrable that when churches work together, they are able to accomplish much more than when they work independently. The results of the Billy Graham crusades are evidence of the power of unity.

A recent survey we conducted found that only 3 percent of the churches in this country consistently work in cooperation with nearby churches that have similar missions or strategies toward jointly accomplishing their goals. Just 3 percent. Although churches are not to be in competition with each other, the practice of the Bodies of faith suggests that we see ourselves as fighting each other for the right to win over certain people. How abundantly foolish. Perhaps we must rectify errant perspectives on evangelism and church unity before we will really see the churches of our nation explode with the healing power of God.

What does your church do in conjunction with nearby churches to reach the unreached? How often do you interact formally with representatives from other churches to avoid duplication of effort and thus a waste of resources? What kind of unifying events are held between churches? What kinds of evangelistic efforts are conducted jointly among a variety of local churches? What have you learned regarding evangelism from the efforts of people in other congregations in your community? Is unified outreach with other churches on your agenda for this year?

## CELEBRATION OF THE VICTORIES

We're all human, which means that, among other things, we need to be recognized for a job well-done and encouraged when things go poorly. Astoundingly, few churches ever grant public or private recognition to the people who devote themselves to carrying out the central mandates of the churches through evangelism. This, too, says something about the ability of the institutional church to maintain a core of committed, energized, enthusiastic evangelizers.

Can public recognition become excessive? Certainly, just as the use of the charismatic gifts can sometimes get out of control or a pastor's sermons can run too long. But that does not mean we discard the entire process. Evangelizers are fulfilling a vital portion of the church's task. They should receive tangible forms of appreciation from the church. And what does it say about the Church if we do not feel a huge degree of gratitude for people's determination to make Christ known, or if we do not feel proud to be part of a group of believers who are committed to fulfilling the Great Commission?

How do you express your thanks to those who evangelize? Recognition dinners? Annual banquets at which the evangelizers are allowed to briefly share what their efforts have meant to them? Congregational applause at special meetings or Sunday services? A personal letter from the pastor? A gift certificate? We have found that as long as the expression is sincere, personal and not routinized, the mode of expression is less important than the message that people care, that they are praying, that they support us in this battle.

# PREPARING FOR A NEW ERA

As we enter the third millennium since the birth of Christ, the societal changes that swarm around us are almost incomprehensible. People need the help the Church can provide, evangelistically and in other, more mundane but significant terms.

Experience shows us that we cannot continue to perceive evangelism as we have in the past, nor can we afford to give up on evangelism as the heart of our ministries. For churches to remain key players in the evangelistic landscape, though, it will require new ways of thinking, fortified commitment to bold and risky forms of outreach and a devotion to prayer and to people in this new age for ministry.

## FACTORS THAT MAY HINDER A CHURCH'S EVANGELISTIC EFFORTS

- The absence of vision for church-based evangelism;
- The lack of churchwide ownership of evangelism as a core value and activity;
- The absence of churchwide prayer for evangelistic efforts;
- A lack of significant relationships with nonbelievers;
- An attitude of disinterest in non-Christians;
- The goal of facilitating decisions rather than conversions;
- Too much reliance upon the pastor to make evangelism happen;
- Not enough strong leadership by the pastor in evangelism;
- The absence of a strategic plan for outreach;
- No accountability for meeting evangelistic goals and standards;
- The inability to change from existing methods to more effective methods;
- Poor-quality ministry activities;
- Having only one entry point for nonbelievers;
- Inadequate training of evangelizers;
- Allocating responsibility without giving authority;
- Failure to celebrate stellar efforts, obedience to God's call and His blessings;
- Division among churches.

# 9

# RESTORING EVANGELISTIC POWER OF INDIVIDUALS

Although the local church is involved in the battle to defeat the forces of evil, every believer has been called by Christ to do whatever he or she can to lead non-Christians, through the enabling of the Holy Spirit, into God's eternal presence.

But as we have seen in earlier chapters, this opportunity is not easy to exploit. Satan and his minions are armed for battle and are arrayed against us in our efforts to restore everlasting life to the souls of unregenerate people. The war in which we are engaged is the ultimate action thriller, but with a twist: We know who wins the war, and we can increase the margin of victory through dedicated service to God, through obedient, intelligent, relentless evangelism.

One of the challenges, of course, is to recruit more people who love Christ and who will share that love with the nonbelievers of America through persistent outreach efforts. In earlier chapters, we considered the state of evangelism in the United States today, and the roles that individual believers play in that state of affairs. In this chapter, let me briefly discuss a few aspects you and I must address to enhance the quality of our personal evangelistic forays.

## CLEANING UP OUR ACT

One of the scariest insights we discovered through our interviews with evangelizers is that a large proportion of them possess spiritual beliefs that are unbiblical. This is frightening because evangelizers pass along what they believe as if it were truth. Consequently, we have a nation of well-meaning believers who are sharing the gospel with nonbelievers but who are also sharing heresy (i.e.. incorrect theology and doctrine).

## BAD THEOLOGY

For instance, among the adults who have shared their faith in the past year:

- One-quarter do not believe that the Bible is accurate in all that it teaches.
- One-third contend that if people are generally good or do enough good things for others during their lives, they will earn a place in heaven, thus negating the necessity of God's grace.
- Four out of every 10 evangelizers believe it does not matter what religious faith a person follows because all faiths teach similar lessons about life.
- One-fourth acknowledge that Jesus made mistakes.

These statistics are just the tip of the iceberg regarding the widespread problem within the Church of bad theology embraced by the most committed people. This profile of the beliefs of the evangelizers helps explain why so many people who commit their lives to Christ possess such an impure blend of beliefs. This data also underscores one major reason half of the people who regularly attend churches have yet to accept Christ as their Savior.

We also found that among people who call themselves Christian, attend a Christian church and share their faith with nonbelievers, *only 67 percent of the evangelizers are truly Christians.*

The issue goes even deeper than spreading bad theology and doctrine. Part of the challenge is also to provide nonbelievers with a complete and accurate introduction to Christian theology.  Our assessment of the message communicated by many evangelizers is that it majors on the positive without acknowledging some of the harsh realities.

In particular, we found that many evangelizers are happy to talk about the good news without providing its context (i.e., we serve a holy God who cannot tolerate sin and will cast His wrath upon those who commit sin without remorse and repentance). Most Christians cannot possibly be explaining the role of God's law in the salvation process because less than half of them even know the contents of the law. As Hosea 4:6 instructs us, it is absurd to believe that human beings will repent because of our inability to uphold the Mosaic law when we don't know what the law commands.

As Paul told Timothy, the law is a vital part of telling people what they are repenting for, of helping them to understand sin and righteousness and of moving people to understand the true significance of grace (see 1 Tim. 1:8-9). In more recent times, Charles Finney contended that unless we use an understanding of the Mosaic law as the context for salvation by grace, we run the risk of making false converts—the condition that runs rampant in our nation today.

We live in a nation where our desire to feel good has overwhelmed our awareness of the consequences of our actions. We push salvation as a route to eternal comfort and pleasure without realizing that the true value is the eternal avoidance of God's unmitigated wrath. We do not want to encourage people to accept Christ out of guilt, but neither do we want them to see salvation as simply a pleasure-producing gift.

What happens when a person does not feel pleasure from Christianity? It is easy to "backslide" when we are unaware of the consequences. We assume those consequences mean that we will not have pleasure. The American mind-set is: "I'll get my pleasure elsewhere." We do not recognize that our reliance upon Christ is our sole means of escaping the wrath that will bind millions after the Day of Judgment.[1]

For the future of the Christian Body to improve, we must focus upon a comprehensive and accurate set of teachings from the Bible, challenging even the most basic assumptions of religious people and motivating them to diligently evaluate their beliefs against the content of Scripture. We must reshape the ways we enlist, train, send and evaluate evangelizers to prevent spreading the heresies that will divide the Church from within and thus undermine its power and its ability to please God.

## BASIC QUIZ ON FAITH

Have you evaluated your own theological beliefs for their accuracy and sufficiency in sharing truth with people? You might wish to quiz yourself to determine how solid you are on the basics of your faith:

- What are the Ten Commandments? (See Exod. 20:1-17.)
- What is the fruit of the Spirit and how does it relate to the development of a devoted follower of Christ? (See Gal. 5:22,23.)
- Why did God create people? (See Gen. 1:28; Deut. 6:1-6.)
- Why was it necessary for God to send His Son to redeem humankind? (See Rom. 3:21-26.)
- How do we know that Jesus was really God's anointed One? (See Acts 2:14-36.)
- What are the primary roles of the Holy Spirit? (See John 16:13,14; Acts 1:8; 2:4; Rom. 8:26; 1 Cor. 12:4-11; 2 Thess. 2:13; Titus 3:5.)
- What is faith? (See Heb. 11:1.)
- Why did Jesus perform miracles? (See John 20:30,31.)

- Why isn't it enough to simply believe that Jesus is God? (See Rom. 10:6-10; Jas. 2:19.)
- What is the greatest commandment, and why? (See Matt. 22:37-39.)
- Why must a person be "born again"? (See John 3:3.)
- What are some of the key beliefs of a Christian? (Apostle's Creed)

These are just a few of the elementary aspects of our faith you and I need to grasp if we are to exploit the myriad opportunities to effectively share what we believe in the marketplace.

## ASLEEP AT THE WHEEL

Scripture tells us that all authority under heaven has been given to the believers to do God's work until He comes again, in glory, in the final days (see Acts 1:8; 2 Cor. 10:4-8; Titus 2:15). In spite of this awesome promise, coupled with the phenomenal privilege of evangelizing the world, our research clearly indicates that *most Christians never share their faith with another person*. One of the major reasons is complacency.

Alarmingly few believers seem to have a passion to reach out to nonbelievers. The result is a Church that is erratic in pursuing the Great Commission. The problem of too few workers to reap the harvest is not because of a shortage of workers; the problem lies in the lack of interest and commitment of most believers to pitch in and do their share of the work.

Do you recall God's response to the church of Laodicea, described in Revelation 3:15,16? "I know your deeds, that you are neither cold nor hot. I wish you were either one or the other! So, because you are lukewarm—neither hot nor cold—I am about to spit you out of my mouth." Clearly, wimpy Christianity displeases God. When we fail to feel deeply about the impending disaster for millions of our countrymen or to be grieved by the eternal agony awaiting many of our family, friends and acquaintances, God's heart is broken.

Perhaps part of the reason for our failure to evangelize is that we do not fully comprehend the horrors of God's everlasting anger poured out against people who reject His gracious offer of salvation as a gift. For many Americans, the coldhearted approach we take to the rest of society may simply be a reflection of our culture-bound selfishness: We got what we need, so let others get what they need for themselves, by themselves.

Whatever the reason, the question you must answer is: When I stand before God to give an accounting of my life, will He perceive that I have urgently and consistently pursued the means and opportunities to tell others about His grace, or will He describe me as a casual evangelizer?

A battle has no place for casual bystanders who shout encouragement or criticism from the sidelines, nor is it a place for the timid recruits who only get involved when it is unavoidable or when they're not really needed. The spiritual battle is raging. Each of us has a part to play on the frontlines. But, much like salvation is a choice we make, so is engagement in the battle. We will not lose our salvation by failing to tell others what we have found in Christ, but neither will we share in the eternal rewards of helping to fulfill Christ's Great Commission to His followers (see 2 Cor. 5:10).

Do you know any people you care about who are not Christians? What can you do that fits your personality and your capacity to share the gospel with those people during the coming months? What approaches would work for you while conveying the greatest message to those people?

■ ■

WE ARE ASSURED THAT WHEN WE ARE PRAYING FOR THE SALVATION OF OTHERS, GOD WILL HEAR THOSE PRAYERS AND IS PLEASED BY THEM. PRAYER IS OUR POWER SOURCE.

■ ■ ■

You don't need to evangelize the way Billy Graham does it. Chances are, he may not be able to evangelize the way you do either. God created each of us to be unique, and that quality encompasses the ways we communicate our faith to others. If the obstacle is a lack of focus on the eternal outcome of other people or simply feeling unmoved by what might happen to others if they do not dedicate their lives to Jesus, read about God's wrath to better understand what may happen to your friends (see Luke 16:19-31; Rev. 20:10-15).

The issues at hand are our priorities and our commitment to God and to our friends. Our determination to prioritize Christ in our lives by making Him real in the lives of others becomes an irrefutable statement about our faith and the nature of our hearts.

## ON YOUR KNEES

As was noted in the previous chapter, evangelism that occurs without the benefit of extensive and intensive prayer support is crippled. Unless we call upon God through prayer, we are seeking to do His work in our own strength even though we are unable to complete the task. There is no reason, however, to take on this gargantuan challenge without the power of God.

Scripture tells us that we are to devote ourselves to prayer, that God hears the prayers of His people and that He responds to our requests. We are told that we do not get the things we desire because we do not pray and because we do not ask for the right things from God.

We are assured that when we are praying for the salvation of others, God will hear those prayers and is pleased by them. Prayer is our power source. Without prayer, we needlessly limit our ability to affect the souls of humankind (see Prov. 15:8,29; Col. 4:2; Jas. 4:2,3; 5:16).

As you think about the people you know who do not have Christ at the center of their lives, ask God to change their hearts. Plead with God to use you as His agent of reconciliation with those people. Beseech Him to include them in the family of faith. God cares about these people, just as He cares for you and me. When we pray for their salvation and are accessible to God as the instrument of grace needed to bring them to Himself, we are true servants. It is the power of prayer that facilitates the salvation of our spiritually needy friends.

## AN EVANGELIZER! WHO, ME?

One of the most difficult hurdles I had to overcome was the notion that I have been called by God to be an evangelizer. I recognize that I do not have the gift of evangelism, nor will evangelism be my primary ministry. Yet, God prepares relationships, meetings and myriad opportunities for me to nudge people closer to Him.

For a long time, I was not open to thinking of myself as an evangelizer. On occasion, it's still difficult because I know what a schmuck I am. It's hard to believe that God can use me to make other people righteous in His eyes through the sacrifice of Christ on the cross.

Although I do not have statistics to prove this, I believe that many Christians avoid personal evangelism because they do not see themselves as evangelizers. They are happy to use their special gifts of teaching, helping and encouraging. But evangelism appears outside the boundaries of reality to them. They have been called to serve, but their service is in other areas.

When Jesus gave the Great Commission to His followers, it was an uncategorical command to everyone, not just a few who enjoyed evangelism. If you and I are to call Him Lord, then we, too, must accept that evangelism is one of the things we must do. As human beings, certain actions must be taken every day if we wish to stay alive—behaviors such as eating, breathing and drinking. These actions allow us to live physically. In the same way, we are called to act if we wish to remain alive spiritually. Sharing God's love through Christ with others is one of those sustaining requirements (see John 15:16).

Do you accept the fact that God wants to use you as an evangelizer? You may never have the evangelistic notoriety of a Billy Graham or a Charles Finney, but God's calling is about obedience, not productivity. As part of our growth as Christians, we must be willing to follow His leadership.

## OVERCOMING DOUBT AND FEAR

Satan's greatest weapon against evangelism is to instill doubts and fears in the hearts of believers. Sometimes the fears and doubts cause us to question our salvation, the majesty and omnipotence of God, the reality of the Resurrection or the authority and accuracy of the Bible. Often, the fears and doubts are implanted in us to prevent us from sharing the good news with those who so desperately need to hear it and who may be especially open to receiving it at that moment in their lives.

Our interviews have discovered three primary doubts and three primary fears among believers when it comes to evangelism. The major doubts relate to God's power, His plan and His promise. Have you ever doubted that God really has the ability to change the heart of a particular person? You wouldn't be alone if you harbored such a concern. But the evidence shows God's amazing ability to melt the hearts of even the most coldhearted people.

In the New Testament, we see astounding transformations of all kinds of people: the irreligious (Samaritan woman), those who opposed Christ (Saul of Tarsus), the poor (Peter), the rich (Luke, Matthew), the sick (the leper, the hemorrhaging woman, blind Bartamaeus), people of influence (the Ethiopian official, Jairus), even family members (Mary, James). Every kind of person you can name is subject to God's authority. The Bible clearly notes that nothing is exempt from the power and authority of God.

Perhaps you find it hard to believe that God would use you as an evangelizer. I certainly have struggled for years to believe that God would use me and some of my friends for that purpose. One of the mysteries beyond my comprehension is His plan to use people whose lives have been changed by the love of Christ to help turn around the lives of other sinners.

Or maybe the stumbling point is knowing that He will be true to His promises to us regarding evangelism, which takes us into the arena with our fears. The trio of anxieties most likely to prevent us from promoting the gospel are our perceived lack of knowledge, the fear of rejection by those with whom we share and the fear of failure.

A minimal amount of knowledge is, in fact, necessary to be effective as an evangelizer. But what knowledge do we really need? Perhaps no more than we already possess, no matter how much or how little we have. We had enough knowledge to make the decision to follow Christ. It may not take much more than that to be used by God to persuade others that His is the only way to peace and everlasting life.

The Bible gives us additional encouragement by intimating that even if we never share the gospel, a person can know of God's power and majesty simply by reflecting on nature and the Creation (see Rom. 1:21). As you grow in your faith, you absorb some of His truths along the journey, and those practical realities have enhanced your spiritual walk and are most likely to be compelling to others. If you never grasp the intricacies of post-

■ ■

## WHETHER A NONBELIEVER ACCEPTS GOD'S OFFER OF SALVATION IS NOT OUR PROBLEM. THAT'S AN ISSUE INVOLVING GOD, THE HOLY SPIRIT AND THE NONBELIEVER.

■ ■ ■

millennialism, or supralapsarianism or transubstantiation, only a few seminary professors may be upset. Those are not the obstacles that prevent nonbelievers from coming to Christ.

Granted, as you mature as a believer, you should attempt to increase your understanding of the Bible and your faith so that if you encounter people who need more sophisticated replies to their questions, you will be equipped. But one of God's great promises is that He will not give you more than you can handle, nor will He abandon you as you seek to do His will (see 1 Cor. 10:13).

But a second fear, that of rejection, is very real. The Bible tells us that as we promote the cause of Christ, we can expect to be persecuted, reviled and rejected—even by friends and family members. In our culture, rejection is not popular with a person who espouses the supremacy of popularity.

But the bottom-line question it raises is: Whom do you love the most—your friends or God? That may be a difficult answer for some people, but the "right" answer is God. We are called to love Him above all else—not to love Him exclusively, but to love Him more deeply than all others.

In serving God out of our passion for Him, we can expect that some people will be offended, confused and disinterested. But our response must be to maintain Him as our first love and to continue to love and appropriately pursue our other loved ones with His message of love and reconciliation.

Rejection will occur if we are faithful. What should be our response? Like the apostles who were beaten by the Jewish leaders for refusing to stay silent about Jesus, we are to be "rejoicing because [we are counted] worthy of suffering disgrace for the Name" (Acts 5:41).

But what about failure? Our research shows that many Christians do not want to let God down and therefore avoid evangelistic encounters. The data indicates that people are fearful of failure on several levels: failing God, failing their church, failing the people with whom they attempt to share the gospel and failing themselves. That's a heavy burden to bear, enough to stimulate anyone to avoid the potential to fail.

But the key to this perspective is to recognize that God views evangelistic failure as refusal to tell the world about His glory and His plans for people. Whether a nonbeliever accepts His offer of salvation is not our problem. That's an issue involving God, the Holy Spirit and the nonbeliever. Our responsibility is to go and tell. We can only pray for people and inform them of the truth. We cannot convert them. That takes more power than we could ever hope to muster.

So what is holding you back from sharing God's desire to love others as He loves you? Cast the fears and doubts aside and go for it! Unlike a surgeon, whose reputation and professional career depend upon skill at identifying the medical problem and performing an operation that will restore the person to full health, we have only to tell the unhealthy patient about the cure. When the time and circumstances are right, God will perform the surgery.

## REACHING A LONELY NATION

Sociologists have described America as the loneliest nation on the face of the earth. Our research suggests they may be right. Although we live in close proximity to tens of thousands of people and probably come in contact with hundreds of people every week, most of us have few real friends, few true confidants.

Research among Christians has found that we have an added difficulty in our lives: We tend to associate with other Christians and thus have few significant relationships with nonbelievers. We struggle with evangelism because we are isolated from the very people God has called us to influence. For most Christians, developing meaningful, authentic relationships with non-Christians will be an act of intent, not an act of chance. We probably will have to look for or creatively make opportunities to encounter and interact with nonbelievers.

Do you know someone who is not a Christian and you would enjoy being with that person? What places do you frequent where you might be more sensitive to meeting new people and befriending them (e.g., health club, adult education classes, neighborhood or condo association meetings)? How often do you pray for opportunities to meet new people you might someday have the privilege of introducing to Jesus Christ? Be proactive on this. Jesus did not wait for people to come to Him. The apostles were not stuck in one place. The biblical model we have is one of believers actively pursuing chances to engage with nonbelievers.

## EVANGELISM TRAINING

A large proportion of the Christians who do not evangelize contend that they are just not prepared for anything that taxing or sophisticated. The concern relates to having received little or no training in evangelism, having no understanding of other faith systems as a basis for conversing intelligently about Christianity in relation to other religions, or not being a capable communicator.

Have you sought out training in evangelism? When Christians from other nations come to the United States, they are blown away by the myriad training options available. Many churches offer assistance in evangelism, training people in the basics. Seminaries and Bible colleges offer courses and many now offer "distance education" opportunities, through which you may complete course work at home and interact by telephone, mail or computer with your instructor.

Several dozen parachurch ministries (e.g., Billy Graham Evangelistic Association, InterVarsity, Campus Crusade) put on outreach seminars across the country. Some of these ministries offer training conferences or "evangelistic boot camps." Hundreds of books are published each year about the practice of evangelism. Videotape training sessions, audiotape sessions and now CD-ROM training sessions are also available.

One of the most overlooked forms of evangelism training is to be mentored by a mature Christian who is involved in evangelism and has a rich desire to involve other people in sharing their faith. This was the primary model used in the Early Church. Notice that the church in Jerusalem did not have training classes, guidebooks or step-by-step programs for outreach. The approach was taught by Jesus: be among the people, live a righteous life, talk about truth from God's perspective and encourage people to take advantage of God's offer of salvation. In the process, develop future evangelizers by operating as a team, where one goes from being the master evangelizer to the mentor, evaluating and assisting an apprentice. Today, we have thousands of church leaders (professional clergy and laity) who have a burning passion for evangelism and are often willing to mentor others.

Evangelism training, then, is readily available. All it takes is time, desire and a bit of effort on your part. You will likely discover that in the course of such training you will learn more about the typical objections of nonbelievers, especially in relation to what other religions believe and what they say about Christianity. Again, this is truly a matter of your commitment to acquire the necessary information or skills for involvement in evangelism.

Communicating effectively is a matter of individual style and capacity. Perhaps the best advice I have received is to simply be myself when telling others about Christ. Memorized presentations, theological arguments and fancy logic may work for some people, but it does not work for me. That does not make me any less useful to God as an evangelizer. In my own inexact and imperfect way, I can tell other people what God has done for me, what I know He would like to do for them and what they can do to accept His offer.

One of the core axioms of effective communication is to be simple. People do not want a complex message. The path to salvation is abundantly simple—not easy, of course, but the process itself is simple to comprehend. When I accepted Christ as my Savior, the thing that perplexed me was the simplicity of the act. It surprised me so much that I had to have time to consider whether something so wonderful as eternal life and a close relationship with God could be obtained through so simple a transaction. God's offer is simple. We do it justice by communicating it to others in a simple manner.

### DO AS I SAY OR DO AS I DO?

In an overstimulated society such as ours, we screen out most of the messages that are sent our way. Every day we encounter more than 2,000 commercial messages, yet less than 2 percent of them actually penetrate and lodge themselves in our consciousness. We automatically filter out every message that seems irrelevant or that seems internally inconsistent.

Evangelistic messages receive the same treatment. If we do not present the gospel in ways that are contextualized, people will assume Christianity is an impractical, irrelevant faith, something they do not need. If we present the message strategically, though, and people can identify ways the faith could be valuable to them, they take the message seriously.

At that point, however, the messenger becomes a potential issue. Is the person who is telling about forgiveness and salvation through acceptance of Christ a person whose life bears the evidence of a spiritual renewal? Does the messenger live like someone who has been forgiven and now has a new perspective on life?

In a society as skeptical as ours, if our lives do not parallel the wondrous transformation that we are proclaiming to the nonbeliever, our credibility is eliminated and the message will not receive a fair hearing. We do the nonbeliever and God a tremendous disservice if we do not get our lives together sufficiently to raise the curiosity of the nonbeliever.

How has your life changed as a result of your decision to follow Christ? When people watch you—and believe me, once you let on publicly that you are a Christian, you will be scrutinized—will they see a sinner trying to follow God's law while relying solely upon His grace, or a religious person cashing in on a free gift, but otherwise unchanged? If your lifestyle contradicts your verbal presentation of God's offer, don't expect to bear much fruit as an evangelizer. If anything, God may protect non-Christians from you.

### BEEN THERE, DONE IT

On an assembly line, you do your assigned task, minute as it might be in the scope of the product being assembled, and leave the rest in the hands of others. But evangelism is not an assembly-line product. Once you become involved in the process, you cannot afford to assume that someone else will pick up from wherever you left off. If you are involved in evangelism, you are in it for the long haul. And you are called to take good care of the people you have been given the privilege to share your faith.

The apostle Paul was a master at sticking with it. He would go back to the community forum day after day and speak with the skeptics and the curious, presenting information, answering questions, asking questions, and praying for them and with them.

Jesus was no different. Upon His initial encounter with each of His disciples, it is apparent that they had no clue who He was, what He expected of them or what precious gift He offered. It took months of intense ministry before Peter was able to identify Jesus as the Savior they had been awaiting (see Matt. 16:17,18). Others in the group undoubtedly took longer to get the point. But what if Jesus had done His evangelistic routine and went off in search of new, unreached people, leaving the disciples to ponder among themselves the significance of what He had said and done? Would they have caught on? Probably not.

In this lifestyle of caring and sharing by Jesus and Paul we have an example to follow. Evangelism is more than just proclaiming the Word. It requires loving people long enough and sincerely enough so that they can hear the Word, grapple with it and ultimately make an informed decision regarding what to do about what they heard.

A major disaster in America is Christians assuming that hit-and-run evangelism is adequate. You and I are called to facilitate a reasonable decision by those with whom we share. We have to be there to answer questions, to probe their thoughts, to encourage them and to help them once they reach a verdict. As the children's rhyme says, "We show we care by being there."

## You Matter in God's Plan

The sinners of America have no hope without Christ. And they are not likely to be brought to faith in Christ through institutions or events, by books or TV programs. You are their best chance of helping them escape the clutches of hell. We have the daunting privilege of ushering undeserving people into God's eternal presence.

Much like our decision regarding where to spend eternity, we have the ability to choose to serve God through personal evangelism or to turn our backs on such service. Unlike our decisions regarding our own salvation, though, this choice will effect the lives of other people. Make the choice carefully.

NOTE

1. Ray Comfort, a New Zealand evangelist, has prepared an excellent presentation on how we may not be providing nonbelievers with a complete understanding of why they should turn to Christ. His presentation, "Hell's Best Kept Secret," is available on audiotape from Mr. Comfort at P.O. Box 1172, Bellflower, CA 90706.

# 10

# WHERE'S THE BEEF?

Before I began writing this book, I was filled with anticipation. I was anxious to focus on the unknown, to be the first to share the exciting discovery of evangelistic success stories that could serve as the springboard to a new era of profound victories for Christ.

I had done my homework, spending nearly two years and tens of thousands of dollars researching evangelism. I had prayed that God would allow me to bless His people by communicating new paths that He has opened for us to travel, to alert the evangelistic leaders of the nation to the waves of the future and to provide some impetus for pursuing those new directions with gusto.

Now, many days and hundreds of pages later, I feel like my balloon of excitement has been deflated. Here we are, at the end of this journey, and I wanted to shout, "Here it is, colleagues in Christ, the latest, the most effective, the unexpected route to evangelistic impact as we enter the new millennium together!" I truly wanted to be able to share new strategies and novel concepts for outreach.

As we near the end of the journey, the bottom line is not what I expected. It is not "I bet you don't know about this strategy yet" or even "This is what all of the hot churches are doing." How could I have known that the real insight to emerge from this study would be as old as Solomon's wisdom: "There is nothing new under the sun" (Eccles. 1:9).

## NEW MODELS ARE NOT SO NEW

So what are the "new models" for evangelism?

Seeker services? Today's seeker strategies are simply updated versions of Jesus' mountainside chats with the crowds or Paul's interactive encounters in the marketplace with the Gentiles.

Socratic evangelism? Jesus initiated evangelism by dialogue. Paul mastered the art. Throughout the ages, many Christians have built churches and outreach ministries on the foundation of Socratic discourse.

What is innovative and promising then? Evangelistic events? Street-corner preaching? Broadcast evangelism? Prayer outreach? Affinity-group meetings? Cell groups? Community development and welfare?

New models? No, nothing is new under the sun.

I had been snared by one of the seductive but erroneous notions promoted in our culture: To be on the cutting edge, something has to be newer, bigger, flashier, more complex. Also erroneous is the belief that the future will be dominated by those people who are the most innovative. To be the best, they will have to be the most unusual, the most creative, the most energetic, the biggest risk-takers.

The truth is that there are no new models for evangelism because we do not *need* new models for evangelism. We only need to understand the theology, the heart and the passion of Jesus Christ as exemplified for us in His ministry. We must be sensitive to the people we are called to reach, true to the principles given to us in Scripture and committed to reaching people with the love of Christ through personal commitment and persistence.

Mind-boggling revivals have occurred throughout history not because of innovation but because of radical obedience to the call to evangelize. Evangelism is effective when people do whatever is necessary to reach the unreached, rather than maintain traditions and accept outdated assumptions for the sake of continuity. Effective evangelism is not about programs, methods or techniques. It is about people who love Christ, about loving other people in the name of Christ.

As it turns out, Nike uses a promotional slogan that should be the Church's evangelistic motto: Just do it!

## NOT A WASTED EFFORT

So I have had to reflect on what this experience and its product, this book, have taught me. First, I have had to realign my expectations to parallel God's. He is interested in changing people, not innovative processes. Second, I have discovered the peace of knowing that God is at work in our culture today, and His methods are more important than the clever strategies we may devise. If we understand our target audience well enough to create a unique approach, He probably will bless the effort if we share His heart to shatter the bubble of complacency and unawareness that keeps tens of millions of people from knowing God.

Upon more careful reflection, then, I feel good about this journey we have pursued together. Our exploration of the past, present and future state of evangelism in America has provided us with useful insights and benefits. We should be encouraged to know that a church does not have to be a megachurch to generate effective evangelism. It's heartening to realize how much evangelistic activity is taking place. We do not need to generate the effort so much as we need to focus existing efforts to create deeper impact. It is exciting to understand the extraordinary magnitude of the opportunities available to us in our backyards, a chance for tremendous influence if we are willing to take the Great Commission seriously.

It is helpful to realize that our culture is really not that much different from the one Jesus turned upside down during His three years of public ministry. It also is valuable to understand what the people who have left the Church are seeking from a religious faith. We have the answers. Now, if we can apply them to the questions the nonbelievers are asking in a contextualized manner, we will witness tremendous results for Christ.

This study has raised more than a few challenges, which we must take seriously if we really care to serve Christ. For instance, we must make key distinctions and respond to them: hearing the gospel versus mere exposure to it, facilitating conversions rather than transient decisions, ministering out of passion for souls rather than a sense of forced obligation to God, and relying upon strategic activities rather than mindless, routine tradition.

Each of us must reflect on what these and the other challenges mean in terms of how we engage in evangelism. For instance, the study has certainly raised the issue of contextualization without compromise as a crucial item. Understanding, differentiating and integrating the evangelistic roles and opportunities of the Church and the individual are significant. Preparing evangelizers for accurate and relevant presentations of the gospel is another central concern. Establishing means of assessment and accountability is another.

Many lessons can be learned about evangelism by studying the efforts of people and of ministries. One lesson is that we do not have to be extraordinarily creative to make a difference. We need integrity, sensitivity, commitment, perseverance—and the blessing of God.

## THE END OF THE MATTER

On the one hand, my initial expectations have been dashed. Innovation is not the key. The cutting edge isn't all that distant from the routine. The future may not be all that different from the past.

On the other hand, I thank God for the simple truths and realities related to effective evangelism today. Sinners accept Jesus Christ as their Savior because He blesses our obedience in sharing the gospel and in waiting for

His perfect timing. If we can filter out the distractions and can focus on knowing, loving and serving God, He can use us to our greatest potential.

Time is of the essence, but as Solomon also told us, there is a time for everything. If we can simply devote ourselves to doing the work of ambassadors of Christ, He will see to the results.

# 11

# STANDING ON THE PROMISES OF GOD

Thankfully, we do not have to evangelize the world on our own power, intelligence, natural ability or righteousness. We do so on the basis of God's calling and God's provision. It is solely on the basis of His presence in our lives and His ability to work through us that we may influence the lives of the people we encounter.

You and I have a responsibility to share the love of Christ with others, seeking to introduce them to the living Savior. In the process of fulfilling that responsibility we can lean on Him for wisdom, power, discernment and guidance toward helping people and pleasing God.

More than that, we can recall and stand firm on the promises He made to us regarding our spiritual development and our ability to touch others on His behalf. When we share His message with others, we invariably grow in that process. Sometimes our hearts mature as we learn to love a bit more deeply, to be touched a bit easier by the plight of the spiritually desperate.

And we may become more sensitive to the nature of God's love for us and the incredibly sophisticated world He has created, and become more aware of the roles we play in that intricate reality. At other times, the act of telling people about Christ may simply deepen our faith in our heavenly Father because we hear anew the story of how He sacrificed His own flesh and blood for ours.

As you seek to obey God's mandate to love others as He loves us, you cannot help but be struck by some of His daunting promises. God said, for example, that sharing the good news will not make us universally popular. God told us that when we become committed to Him, we can count on Satan to turn up his wrath a few notches. Such promises raise the question: "With a friend like this, who needs an enemy?"

But on the other side of the coin rest an array of amazing, exhilarating, unique promises God has made to us that represent an enduring source of empowerment and love, even when our best efforts seem to move us backward. As a launching pad as an effective evangelizer, serving the only spiritual force in the universe that is worth knowing and promoting, remember these words of blessing and encouragement God gave to you and me.

## THE CALL TO SHARE THE GOOD NEWS

• A person's final words are always well chosen and important. This was true for Jesus, too, as He was about to leave His 11 remaining disciples for the last time. In the famous charge we call the "Great Commission," He instructed them about their—and our—most important pursuit.

> Therefore go and make disciples of all nations, baptizing them in the name of the Father and of the Son and of the Holy Spirit, and teaching them to obey everything I have commanded you. And surely I am with you always, to the very end of the age (Matt. 28:19,20).

• We will have days when we wish for a speedy end to our earthly trials and tribulations. But God's plan will not be thwarted by the day-to-day crises, nor His Word stopped by human effort or by Satan. Part of God's promise is that all people must hear the gospel. And so they shall.

> And the gospel must first be preached to all nations (Mark 13:10).

• As believers in Jesus Christ, each of us becomes a priest of the Christian faith. A priest has certain obligations, one of which is to proclaim the good news to all those who need that healing Word.

> Because of the grace God gave me to be a minister of Christ Jesus to the Gentiles with the priestly duty of proclaiming the gospel of God, so that the Gentiles might become an offering acceptable to God, sanctified by the Holy Spirit (Rom. 15:15,16).

• Sometimes you may wonder if anyone is left who has not yet heard the gospel. But the ways of men can be deceiving. We are to be diligent in our efforts to ensure that all have heard—really heard—the good news. Some who claim to be Christian may not be; others we assume are believers may not truly know Christ.

> "The kingdom of heaven is like a man who sowed good seed in his field. But while everyone was sleeping, his enemy came and

sowed weeds among the wheat, and went away. When the wheat sprouted and formed heads, then the weeds also appeared....'Let both grow together until the harvest. At that time I will tell the harvesters: First collect the weeds and tie them in bundles to be burned; then gather the wheat and bring it into my barn'" (Matt. 13:24-26,30).

"Not everyone who says to me, 'Lord, Lord,' will enter the kingdom of heaven, but only he who does the will of my Father who is in heaven....I will tell them plainly, 'I never knew you. Away from me, you evildoers!'" (Matt. 7:21-23).

• We share the good news because it is God's will and it brings Him pleasure and honor. We may experience the same joy in the victories in which we play a role as those who see the unfolding of human drama from the heavens.

"I tell you, there is rejoicing in the presence of the angels of God over one sinner who repents" (Luke 15:10).

• One of Satan's greatest ploys is to persuade us that we are not worthy of serving a holy God, that we are incapable of leaving our frailties long enough to lead others into the presence of God. It is a deceit. God has called us to be His channel to the hearts and minds of the unrepentant.

"Therefore I tell you that the kingdom of God will be taken away from you and given to a people who will produce its fruit" (Matt. 21:43).

• Good people may not see heaven. Folks who have committed themselves to serving other people may live in everlasting torment. The key is not our works but God's gracious offer of salvation through our acceptance of Jesus as our Savior.

"I tell you the truth, no one can see the kingdom of God unless he is born again" (John 3:3).

• To be a Christian is to be humbled. A vital reflection of humility is to abandon pride and ego and to admit that we are wholly subject to the will and judgment of God. Evangelism is a tangible means of proclaiming God to be our Master and to satisfy His ordinance that we should serve Him by serving those who are not worthy to be served—just as Jesus served the disciples.

"I have set you an example that you should do as I have done for you. I tell you the truth, no servant is greater than his master, nor is a messenger greater than the one who sent him. Now that you know these things, you will be blessed if you do them" (John 13:15-17).

## THE PROMISE TO PROVIDE FOR OUR NEEDS

• Evangelistic activity places us in the middle of the spiritual battlefield. But God will not leave us there unprotected. He promises to shield us from the attacks of the evil one.

But the Lord is faithful, and he will strengthen and protect you from the evil one" (2 Thess. 3:3).

"In this world you will have trouble. But take heart! I have overcome the world" (John 16:33).

• Sometimes the obstacles will seem overwhelming. We will feel over-matched, outwitted, likely to fail. But the key is that God fights the battles for us, through us. We need only be obedient and watch Him do the unfathomable.

"Be strong and courageous. Do not be afraid or terrified because of them, for the Lord your God goes with you; he will never leave you nor forsake you" (Deut. 31:6).

"If you love me, you will obey what I command. And I will ask the Father, and he will give you another Counselor to be with you forever—the Spirit of truth" (John 14:15-17).

• Whatever it takes, God is capable of providing the resources to complete the job. In working through us, He becomes a partner, and He promises to give us what we need to be effective agents of the gospel.

He who began a good work in you will carry it on to completion until the day of Christ Jesus (Phil. 1:6).

## THE PROMISE OF EFFECTIVENESS

• We are not wasting our time looking for a needle in a haystack. People need Christ, and they need somebody to love them into the Kingdom.

"The harvest is plentiful but the workers are few" (Matt. 9:37).

• God truly desires for all people to love Him and to pursue everlasting life. Everyone we encounter is a viable prospect for deliverance from sins.

> He is patient with you, not wanting anyone to perish, but everyone to come to repentance (2 Pet. 3:9).

• Only one warrior in the battle for people's souls will emerge victorious: the Lord. Every battle has ebbs and flows, but we must remain confident that the Creator is in full control.

> "I will build my church, and the gates of Hades will not overcome it" (Matt. 16:18).

• If we were to handpick those who deserve to enter the gates of heaven, we might be hard-pressed to list any candidates. Our job, however, is not to judge others or to qualify them by using our criteria. If we faithfully share the good news with anyone—for we are all sinners—God will handle the rest.

> When the disciples heard this, they were greatly astonished and asked, "Who then can be saved?" Jesus looked at them and said, "With man this is impossible, but with God all things are possible" (Matt. 19:25,26).

## THE PROMISE TO REWARD US

• When we prove that we can handle a bit of responsibility and challenge, God will allow us to take on more in His service. Our efforts do not go unseen or without appropriate reward.

> "'Well done, good and faithful servant! You have been faithful with a few things; I will put you in charge of many things. Come and share your master's happiness!'" (Matt. 25:21).

• Once we invite Christ to be our Lord and Savior, our salvation is covered by His sacrificial grace. But as we endeavor to obey His commands during our remaining time on earth, we may also earn heavenly rewards for our diligence in pursuing the matters of God.

> "For the Son of Man is going to come in his Father's glory with his

angels, and then he will reward each person according to what he has done" (Matt. 16:27).

• Every day we have opportunities to pursue various outcomes. God promises us that if we reject the temptations and the lures of the world in favor of serving Him and pursuing His ends, we will someday reap the benefits of that choice.

The wicked man earns deceptive wages, but he who sows righteousness reaps a sure reward (Prov. 11:18).

The eternal fate of the world rests in our hands. God has chosen to use you and me as messengers to carry the good news to the world that Jesus did not die in vain, but for the sake of the undeserving. Be bold and courageous, be wise and sensitive, be diligent and strategic. We have the privilege of telling people about Jesus Christ!

# APPENDICES

# LIST OF CHURCHES INTERVIEWED

The following is a list of the churches we interviewed for this book.

Beaverton Foursquare Church
Beaverton, Oreg.

Calvary Community Church
Westlake Village, Calif.

Community Baptist Church
Alta Loma, Calif.

Christian Fellowship Baptist
Church
College Park, Ga.

Crystal Cathedral Hispanic
Ministry
Garden Grove, Calif.

Deliverance Evangelistic Church
Philadelphia, Pa.

Emmanuel Baptist Church
McAllen, Tex.

Evergreen Baptist Church
Rosemead, Calif.

Faith United Methodist Church
Boynton Beach West, Fla.

Fellowship of Las Colinas
Irving, Tex.

First Baptist Church
Leesburg, Fla.

First Baptist Church
Snellville, Ga.

First Baptist Church
Woodstock, Ga.

Franklin Avenue Baptist Church
New Orleans, La.

Hebron Baptist Church
Dacula, Ga.

Horizon Christian Fellowship
San Diego, Calif.

Iglesia ACYM of Queens
Jamaica, N.Y.

Korean Central Presbyterian Church
Vienna, Va.

Lake Avenue Congregational
Hispanic Congregation
Pasadena, Calif.

Mandarin Baptist Church of Los
Angeles
Alhambra, Calif.

Mecklenburg Community Church
Charlotte, N.C.

New Venture Christian Fellowship
Oceanside, Calif.

People's Park Reformed Church
Patterson, N.J.

Perimeter Church
Atlanta, Ga.

Rolling Hills Covenant Church
Rolling Hills Estate, Calif.

San Jose Chinese Alliance Church
San Jose, Calif.

Third Street Church of God
Washington, D.C.

Trinity United Church of Christ
Chicago, Ill.

University Carillon United Methodist Church
Oviedo, Fla.

Vineyard Christian Fellowship
Cincinnati, Ohio

West Angeles Church of God in Christ
Los Angeles, Calif.

Willow Creek Community Church
South Barrington, Ill.

Wooddale Church
Eden Prairie, Minn.

**2**

# CONGREGATIONAL EVANGELISTIC PASSION ASSESSMENT QUESTIONNAIRE

## EVALUATING YOUR CHURCH

If you are interested in discerning how evangelistic your church is, you may wish to fill out the following simple questionnaire. Compare your responses to those listed for the evangelistic congregations in America. This is not an exact, foolproof measure, but simply a means of estimating how your church compares to others we have studied that are intensely focused upon evangelism.

1. How many new members or regular participants attended your church this year, compared to last year? What proportion of those newcomers are at your church in response to accepting Christ as their Savior directly because of the evangelistic efforts of your church or the people in your church?
2. What proportion of your annual budget is allocated to evangelistic activities and expenses?
3. In the plans and strategies outlined for your church's ministry for this year, how prominent is the focus upon evangelism, as determined by:

   a. Events and programs designed to reach out to nonbelievers;
   b. Hiring additional staff who have an evangelistic inclination;

c. The training events available to the congregation for preparation and support in evangelistic activities;

d. The frequency with which the church prays, as a congregation, for nonbelievers to accept Christ as their Savior and for the efforts of church participants who are active in evangelism;

e. The consistency with which the pastor expresses public interest in and support of evangelistic activity;

f. The emphasis upon reaching children and youth with the gospel.

## CONTEXT FOR COMPARISON:

Question 1: In the evangelistic churches, we find that 20 percent or more of the growth is attributable to conversions, rather than to transfer or biological growth.

Question 2: Churches that prioritize evangelism tend to spend at least 10 percent of their annual budgets on local outreach.

Question 3: Evangelistic churches tend to (a) incorporate an evangelistic thread in every program or event; (b) only hire staff who have an evangelistic focus, regardless of their areas of specialization or primary responsibilities; (c) offer two or more training events for the laity during the year to better equip and support them in outreach; (d) pray every week during the worship services and have a prayer team that prays specifically for efforts at reaching non-Christians; (e) the pastor regularly (at least once a month) expresses encouragement to the church Body to focus on outreach; and (f) the primary goal of the youth workers in the church is to see kids accept Christ as their Savior.

## EVALUATING YOUR PERSONAL MINISTRY

In examining the ministry of evangelists, some commonalities indicate the heart and focus of people who take the Great Commission most seriously. Although most of these people do *not* have the spiritual gift of evangelism, they do embrace a spiritual calling, given to all believers, to promote Jesus Christ to those who are not His disciples. You may wish to reflect on your ministry in light of how those who consistently evangelize might answer these questions. Again, this is just a rough estimate of where you stand.

1. How many non-Christian friends do you have?
2. How many times have you shared the gospel with a nonbeliever during the past 12 months?

3. Which of the following gets you most excited: seeing a nonbeliever accept Jesus Christ as Savior; learning new truths about your faith; helping your church become more organized or efficient; or meeting new people through the church?

4. How many nonbelievers do you pray for, by name, every day, asking God to save them?

5. When you enter into a conversation with someone and have the opportunity to express your faith to them, are you most likely to explain your beliefs or to hold off until another conversation in the future?

6. Do you always share your faith in the same way or do you use a variety of approaches and methods in communicating what and why you believe?

7. When you share your faith with a nonbeliever, how confident are you that the person will accept Christ as Savior?

8. If your church significantly changed its style of services to attract more non-Christians and have a better chance of reaching them, how supportive of such a change would you be?

9. How do you feel after sharing your faith with a nonbeliever: embarrassed, fearful, excited, indifferent, fatigued, alive or angry?

## CONTEXT FOR COMPARISON:

Question 1: Most Christians who are serious about evangelism consciously develop relationships with non-Christians so they will have an opportunity, at an appropriate time, to share the gospel.

Question 2: Lay evangelists share the gospel with an average of one nonbeliever every month. The average is probably not as significant, however, as the fact that these people are consistently telling others about Jesus Christ.

Question 3: All of the experiences listed are important and worth rejoicing about. One of the distinctives of lay evangelists, however, is that they would be most likely to get excited about seeing a nonbeliever accept Jesus Christ as Savior. Yes, they enjoy each of the other outcomes and experiences, but the heart of the lay evangelist leaps for joy when a lost soul finds its way into God's kingdom—especially if they had the privilege of helping that lost soul find the path of salvation.

Question 4: Lay evangelists tend to pray persistently and specifically for nonbelievers.

Question 5: When lay evangelists have the chance to share their faith, they seize the moment; they know that they may never have another opportunity to do so in a comfortable and appropriate setting.

Question 6: The most effective evangelizers recognize that every nonbeliever has different needs, interests, fears and expectations, and therefore needs a customized approach to hearing the gospel. Evangelism is not a one-method-fits-all proposition. Those who reach the most people contextualize their approach.

Question 7: Evangelizers tend to believe that if they share the truth, nobody can resist it for long. They also know, however, that they are called to be obedient rather than to worry about the outcome; that's the role of the Holy Spirit.

Question 8: Those who are evangelistic at heart are more concerned about reaching people than about the discomforts brought on by change.

Question 9: For some Christians, sharing their faith is a nightmare. For those people who have truly prayed about being prepared to share their faith, and have released the results to God, evangelistic encounters usually leave them feeling excited, alive and expectant.

# BIBLIOGRAPHY

Aldrich, Joseph. *Life-Style Evangelism*. Sisters, Oreg.: Multnomah Press, 1981.

Barna, George. *The De-Churched American*. Glendale, Calif.: Barna Research Group, Ltd., 1995.

————. *Baby Busters*. Chicago: Northfield Publishing, 1994.

————. *Virtual America*. Ventura, Calif.: Regal Books, 1994.

————. *Turnaround Churches*. Ventura, Calif.: Regal Books, 1993.

————. *Today's Pastors*. Ventura, Calif.: Regal Books, 1993.

————. *User Friendly Churches*. Ventura, Calif.: Regal Books, 1991.

————. *Never on a Sunday*. Glendale, Calif: Barna Research Group, Ltd., 1991.

Coleman, Robert. *The Master Plan of Evangelism*. Grand Rapids, Mich.: Fleming H. Revell Company, 1963.

Draper, Edythe, ed. *Almanac of the Christian World, 1993-1994*. Wheaton, Ill.: Tyndale House Publishers, 1992.

Engel, James, and Norton, Wilbert. *What's Gone Wrong With the Harvest?* Grand Rapids, Mich.: Zondervan Publishing House, 1975.

Frost, S. E. *Basic Teachings of the Great Philosophers*. Garden City, N.Y.: Dolphin Books, 1962.

Graham, Billy, et al. *Choose Ye This Day*. Minneapolis: World Wide Publications, 1989.

Green, Michael. *Evangelism Through the Local Church*. Nashville: Thomas Nelson Publishers, 1992.

Griffin, Em. *The Mind Changers*. Wheaton, Ill.: Tyndale House Publishers, 1976.

Heck, Joel, ed. *The Art of Sharing Your Faith*. Grand Rapids, Mich.: Fleming H. Revell Company, 1991.

Hunter, George. *How to Reach Secular People*. Nashville: Abingdon Press, 1992.

Huston, Sterling. *Crusade Evangelism and the Local Church*. Minneapolis: World Wide Publications, 1984.

Hybels, Bill, and Mittelberg, Mark. *Becoming a Contagious Christian*. Grand Rapids, Mich.: Zondervan Publishing, 1994.

Innes, Dick. *I Hate Witnessing*. Ventura, Calif.: Regal Books, 1983.

Kreeft, Peter. *Socrates Meets Jesus.* Downers Grove, Ill.: InterVarsity Press, 1986.

Montgomery, Jim. *DAWN 2000.* Pasadena, Calif.: William Carey Library, 1989.

Peterson, Jim. *Evangelism for Our Generation.* Colorado Springs: NavPress, 1985.

Pippert, Rebecca. *Out of the Salt Shaker and Into the World.* Downers Grove, Ill.: InterVarsity Press, 1979.

Posterski, Donald. *Reinventing Evangelism.* Downers Grove, Ill.: InterVarsity Press, 1989.

Ratz, Calvin, et al. *Mastering Outreach and Evangelism.* Sisters, Ore.: Multnomah Press, 1990.

Sider, Ronald. *One-Sided Christianity?* Grand Rapids, Mich.: Zondervan Publishing House, 1989.

Silvoso, Ed. *That None Should Perish.* Ventura, Calif.: Regal Books, 1994.

Strobel, Lee. *Inside the Mind of Unchurched Harry and Mary.* Grand Rapids, Mich.: Zondervan Publishing House, 1993.

Wagner, C. Peter. *Church Planting for a Greater Harvest.* Ventura, Calif.: Regal Books, 1990.

———. *Churches That Pray.* Ventura, Calif.: Regal Books, 1993.

———. *Breaking Strongholds in Your City.* Ventura, Calif.: Regal Books, 1993.

Wimber, John. *Power Evangelism.* San Francisco: HarperSanFrancisco, 1985. Reprint, 1992.

# THE BARNA RESEARCH GROUP, LTD.

The Barna Research Group, Ltd. has been providing information and analysis regarding cultural trends and the Christian Church since 1984. The vision of the company is to provide organizations with current, accurate and reliable information in bite-size pieces, at affordable prices, so they may make better decisions. Although Barna Research does not work exclusively for Christian ministries (it has conducted research for TV networks, advertising agencies, financial institutions, universities and other entities), its primary focus is helping Christian ministries become more effective and efficient in carrying out their vision.

Barna Research serves individuals and organizations in three ways. First, the company conducts primary research for clients on topics of interest to the client. Qualitative and quantitative methods may be used, as appropriate, to arrive at a better understanding of the conditions and opportunities that pertain to the client's scope of activity.

Second, the company also conducts syndicated research, which is then released in the form of books, reports, video presentations and audiotapes. Each of these resources is geared to addressing a particular topic of special interest to Christian ministries.

The third service provided by Barna Research is public presentations. Currently, Barna Research sponsors two kinds of seminars: A one-day seminar for church leaders, entitled "Maximizing Your Ministry Impact: Serving Effectively in a Changing Culture," and a one-day intensive seminar for pastors and church staff, entitled "What Effective Churches Have Discovered: New Insights on Ministry in the Late Nineties." Barna Research offers these seminars in a variety of markets around the country.

If you would like to be placed on the mailing list to be informed of new resources available from the Barna Research Group, or to receive a current catalog of resources, please write to us at:

BARNA RESEARCH GROUP, LTD.
P.O. BOX 4152
GLENDALE, CA 91222-0152
(TEL) 818-241-9300
(FAX) 818-246-7684

# More Informative Resources from George Barna.

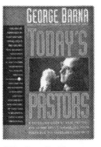

269.2 B259                    90171
Barna, George.
Evangelism that works

DEMCO